KNOW YOUR RIGHTS:
EASY EMPLOYMENT LAW
FOR EMPLOYEES

Know Your Rights:
Easy Employment Law for Employees
By Charles Henter

Copyright © 2013 by Charles Henter.

All rights reserved. No part or portion of this work may be reproduced or transmitted in any form, by any means (including but not limited to electronic, photocopying, recording, or any information retrieval and storage system now known or to be invented) without the written permission of the copyright holder, except by a reviewer who wishes to quote brief passages in connection with a review.

Printed & Published in the United States of America
by Novus Lex LLC, February 2013

Cover by Keith Damiani
Book Design by Novus Lex LLC

PUBLISHED BY
novusLex

Acknowledgements

I am deeply thankful to my wife, Ioline. Not only has she supported me and read through about fifty versions of this book, she is also a fantastic editor. If any mistakes at all remain (or if you think any attempted humor is lame), it is because I did not listen to her and left those things in. I also want to thank my son, Luke. He was my first reader. I assumed that if he could understand this stuff as a thirteen year-old, I was doing something right.

I also want to thank two friends. First, Keith Damiani, who designed my cover and provided helpful feedback; I am very grateful for both. Second, John Davidson, who made invaluable comments and edits to this book.

Finally, I want to thank George Mason University School of Law. GMUSL holds a special place in my heart. It was and is the best school I ever attended, and its faculty and staff did more to educate and inspire me than any other institution. I will be forever thankful.

Dedication

This book is dedicated to my wife and our two sons.
I love them dearly, and always will.

TABLE OF CONTENTS

INTRODUCTION	1
Serious Early Warning Device	3
Disclaimer	5

CHAPTER 1 BASIC AMERICAN RULE OF EMPLOYMENT AT-WILL	7
What is Employment At-Will?	7
Changes to Employment At-Will	13
The Government Says You Can't Fire Me for What I Did, So There	17
Now the Government Says You Can't Treat Me That Way, So Stop!	18
What is a Tort?	20
Sample Employment At-Will Consultation	22

CHAPTER 2 WHEN YOUR EMPLOYER LIES ABOUT YOU (DEFAMATION)	27
What is Defamation?	27
The Employer Has to Communicate the False Fact to Someone	28
You Have to Prove It's False	31
Opinions and Free Speech	31
Can You Prove You Have Been Harmed?	33
Evil Employer Intent	35
Interfering With Your Attempt to Find a New Job	36

CHAPTER 3 JOHNNY BE GOOD: NON-COMPETITION AGREEMENTS	41

CHAPTER 4 DISCRIMINATION	49
What is Discrimination?	49
Not All Discrimination Breaks the Law	50

Bad Things Happen	53
Proving that the Bad Thing Happened Because of a Protected Reason	56
How a Lawyer Looks at Discrimination	61
Other Types of Discrimination	62
Making a Claim of Discrimination	63
Religion Gets Special Treatment ... Sort Of	66

INTERLUDE—TO THE LEGAL SCHOLARS OUT THERE	69

CHAPTER 5 HARASSMENT AND HOSTILE WORK ENVIRONMENT	71
What is Harassment?	71
Is It Always About Sex?	74
An Employer Has a Powerful Defense	76
Reporting Harassment to the EEOC	80

CHAPTER 6 RETALIATION	83
When Are You Protected?	84
You Can Go Too Far	86
So What is Retaliation?	88
Careful, Careful—Retaliation and Reporting Harassment	89

CHAPTER 7 DISABILITIES & ACCOMMODATIONS	93
Do You Have a Disability?	93
What is an Accommodation?	97
How Do You Get an Accommodation?	100
Federal Employees and Disability Discrimination	101
Sick But Not Disabled	101

Chapter 8 Freedom of Speech	105
Private Employees	105
Public Employees	109
Can I Be Fired For Being a Republican? Democrat? Libertarian? Independent? Tea Partier? Bull Moose? Socialist? Statist? Member of the People's Front of Judea?	112

Chapter 9 Employee Privacy	113
Employment File	113
Searches—How Criminal Law Applies to Public Employees	114
Invasion of Privacy	117
You Just Searched What? More on IIED	119
Love, Employment Style—Employee Relationships	120
Privacy in Electronic Information	122
Passwords and Social Media	124

Chapter 10 Quick & Dirty Unemployment Law	127
Looking for Work	128
Quit or Be Fired	129
Bad Employee—Misconduct	131

Chapter 11 When Should You Hire a Lawyer?	133
Top 10 Tips to Employees	135

CHAPTER 12 ONLINE RESOURCES	141
General Resources	141

About the Author	145
Index	147

INTRODUCTION

So, you bought this book because you want to know more about your rights in the workplace, right? Or perhaps you think you are about to get fired and want to protect yourself. Virtually every day, I get a telephone call or email from someone wanting to know if he or she can sue their employer over how they have been treated. You see, I am an employment lawyer. People contact me when they lose their job and want to know if, well, something is their employer's fault. In addition, I have been teaching employment law and discrimination as an Adjunct Professor of Law since 2003.

I decided to write this book because I am sure thousands of workers are out there who want to know about their rights, but are simply not able to afford an attorney to receive even basic information. Of course, a few employment lawyers advertise free consultations, and you might get a chance to actually talk with one of them. While I continue to believe that you get what you pay for, I also know that those free consultations do not really provide an employee with any useful information (it's usually just a meeting in which the lawyer is attempting to determine whether he or she wants to sign you up as a contingency fee client, i.e., he or she is primarily focused on deciding whether he or she can make money off you, while you continue to remain in the dark about your rights and about what is really going on). I hope this book helps people as they mull over their options and decide whether or not to seek the advice of an attorney. In addition, I hope that after reading this book, employees have a better understanding of their rights, and of what an employer can and cannot do.

As a lawyer and professor, I should probably also mention that I have developed three basic rules to help me, and my clients, keep their sanity in this field. I mention these now because it also helps you, the reader, gauge whether the law can help you or not. First Rule: life is not fair. I think we can all agree on the general application of this one. It does lead, however, to the Second Rule: I (and no other lawyer) can make life fair. If you are looking for the law, or a lawyer, to right all the wrongs you have suffered at your job or your life, you are overestimating what the law really does. If you find a lawyer who promises you fairness … run. With very few exceptions, lawyers like that are about to steal your wallet or use you in a public relations event that equals massive advertising for them without much benefit to you. Finally, the Third Rule brings these two together: a lawsuit is not about the truth, it is only about what you can prove.

These three rules are why some people hate lawyers or think that lawyers are cold, calculating, heartless individuals. It may be true that your boss just called you the worst insult in the world and that's why you punched him in the face. However, if we cannot prove he insulted you (such as by using another witness, or by proving he has a history of using such epithets or insulting language), then there is little a lawyer can do to excuse the fact that you just committed a crime. If you can't prove it, you can't use it.

Some people who read this book (I am looking at you, law students) may think that some things I say are not 100% correct in 100% of cases in every

State. You are correct, you get an A. By its nature, this book is not a legal treatise written for legal professionals and meant to cover every nook, cranny, and dusty shadow of the law. Tons of other materials explore the nuances and theories of employment law for lawyers and professors. In fact, I have many of them on my bookshelves—they do look impressive in all that faux leather binding. Instead, this book is meant to be a guide to general employment law for employees. My hope is that my intended audience finds this book and the information it contains helpful.

Also, a careful reader might note that I do not discuss every area in the employment law field. I based this book on the most common problems that employees have when they come to see me. Thus, I chose to focus only on those areas where employees were telling me they really wanted information and advice because it was not easy to find otherwise.

Serious Early Warning Device

Writing this book has been kind of like captaining the *Titanic*. I am trying to chart a course that explains the tips of employment law icebergs to you, while at the same time knowing that below the surface, hidden, sharp dangers are ever present. I sincerely hope that you find the explanations in this book easy to understand and simple—this is my ultimate goal. If, however, you think I am trying to explain all of employment law to you so that you can represent yourself, you misunderstand this book and my intent. This is such an important issue that I will mention it in other ways throughout your reading.

I need to be blunt with you. This book probably explains about five percent of employment law to you. It is meant to be a clear and useful overview of a vast and complex field. Like so much of the law, the general rules are easy to understand, but knowing when those general rules do not apply (or the exceptions to the rules) is immensely complicated. Throw in the additional thousands of regulations that affect employment law (for example, for some laws, it actually matters if you work near a river) and all the possible unique details of every employee's case and, well, I hope you see how this complex area of law only gets more confusing. Yes, I am saying that employment law is extremely complex. The devil is in the details after all.

You might skeptically think that, of course, an employment lawyer would say such things. It certainly benefits lawyers when they claim that the law is complex. I can appreciate such suspicion—you are a person after my own heart. Nevertheless, what I believe is that after reading this book, you will have a little bit of (quality) knowledge to guide you. A little bit of knowledge, however, can be dangerous to people who think they know more than they actually do. If it helps, think of it this way. Assume this book was not about employment law but about basic human anatomy. If you read it and it all made sense, do you think you would be qualified to perform surgery? Of course not. You would, however, be able to make more informed decisions about your health care. And that is precisely why I wrote this book—to help you make better decisions.

In sum, simply knowing some basic rules does not mean you really understand employment law. This is why I wrote Chapter 11 about when to hire a lawyer. Please, if you think your employer might have broken the law, contact an employment lawyer. They (we) really are worth at least the price of a consultation.

Disclaimer

I am afraid I have to get, as my mother might say, all lawyery on you now. Please know that this is just a book and is not meant to be legal advice of any kind. I am writing about the general law in the United States, and focusing a lot on federal law. While I hope that this book provides useful, general information, it cannot and is not meant to give you legal advice. If you have legal questions about a specific situation in your state, please contact a lawyer (preferably an employment lawyer). Buying this book does not make me your lawyer, nor does it create an attorney-client relationship. I think you get it. This is basic information. Hire a professional for specific advice. Get it? Got it? Good.

Chapter 1

Basic American Rule of Employment At-Will

I could begin this book by explaining how the basic American rule of *employment at-will* tracked English law up to the 1780s and how Parliament mucked about with laws four hundred years ago in response to this plague and that plague to create a supply of labor for the rich, and that the basics of American employment law are sort of a response to that system and to the evils of English apprenticeships. I could also say that an evil gnome of a legal scholar created the American rule in the 19th century on a whim just to make individuals advocating for employee rights turn purple-faced with rage in the 21st century (yes, many a modern legal scholar believes something close to this). But I won't do that. I'll save these wonderful details for torturing my students in class. It is enough to say that the general rule in the United States is that people are employed at-will.

What is Employment At-Will?

In an at-will employment system, the employer can generally hire, fire, promote, demote, punish, and just about do whatever it wants to an employee, unless one of two things stop it: a law or an agreement. At the same time, an employee is totally and completely free to walk away from any job at any time. Sounds perfectly balanced, doesn't it? At its most basic level, however, employment at-will is about freedom—freedom for the employer to do what it wants and freedom for the employee to do what he or she wants.

So, an at-will employee can be fired. Okay. For any reason. Got it. Even a stupid one. Yep. Even if it's a terrible business decision. Indeed. Here is an example of at-will employment that I frequently share with my clients. Assume that I am an Evil Employer. I am in a bad mood. I decide that what will really make me happy is to fire an employee. I don't just want to be happy, though. I want to be really happy. Since I am an Evil Employer, my evil logic tells me that I will be happiest if I fire my best, most productive, most profitable, most likeable, and most intelligent employee who has never, ever done anything wrong. So I fire him or her. I can. No one can stop me. That is freedom. That is employment at-will.

Under these gloomy circumstances, you are probably thinking that you sure want to get out of the employment at-will system and get some job security because you are that best, most productive, most profitable, most likeable, and most intelligent employee. Okay. Other than a change in the law (which we will discuss later), the two most common ways for a job not to be at-will is either through a union contract (or collective bargaining agreement as we lawyers refer to them), or a written contract for a specified amount of time. Assuming that you are not a union employee, you might not be employed at-will if you have a contract that says you are an employee who starts on one specific date and ends on another. For example, if you have a contract saying that you were hired as a curtain decorator for Curtains Unlimited from February 1, 2011 to January 31, 2015, you might be a ***term employee*** and not an at-will employee. Your employer may only be able to fire you if it has a good reason, or maybe even a really good reason.

Did I just say you *might* be a term employee but not definitely? Yes. Some courts have decided that at-will employment is such a great thing that to change that basic rule, you have to be super, duper clear about it. So, in some States (hello, Virginia), you will probably need more specific language in the contract saying that the employment is not at-will, and that the employee can only be fired for good or just cause. In these kinds of places, contracts will often have a clause explaining how an employee can be fired (hint: look for a section in your contract called "Termination").

So, what does being a term employee get you? If you happen to be an employee who is not employed at-will, your employer has to have a good reason to fire you. If they don't, then they have broken their agreement with you and you can sue them for breaking that agreement. More importantly, you might be able to get your job back or perhaps the monetary equivalent, plus some other things depending on the actual law in your State.

If you are not an at-will employee, this brings us to the question of how an employer can fire you. Courts and State laws typically use two terms: good cause and just cause. Now, do you remember second grade when your teacher told you that a square is a rectangle, but a rectangle is not a square? That is kind of what good cause and just cause is like. In this case, just cause is the square. Anything that satisfies a "just cause" to fire a person (square) also satisfies a "good cause" (rectangle). However, things that meet the good cause standard do not always meet the just cause standard. I know, it's not terribly clear what good cause and just cause even are yet!

So, let's start with ***just cause***. What is it? Usually, just cause is where the classic line of malfeasance, misfeasance, and nonfeasance lands. At its simplest, malfeasance would be breaking a company rule; nonfeasance would be not showing up to work; and misfeasance would be really screwing up at work. All of these would satisfy just cause. Would making a single mistake at work satisfy just cause? Normally, no. A minor problem would probably not satisfy just cause. However, if you make a series of small mistakes over time, that can result in a "just cause" reason to fire someone. How about if you miss just one day of work without an excuse? Even that can be just cause, because not showing up to work without an excuse is rarely considered a minor mistake. Having that good excuse may save you from being fired. Showing up an hour or so late is more likely to be minor, and would not satisfy just cause.

Good cause is what most States and courts use when determining if a non-at-will employee can be fired. Guess what? Courts sometimes call this ... just cause, and do not think there is any difference between just or good cause (some lawyers think so too). You gotta love the law. At its heart, though, good cause simply means that an employer has to have a decent reason to fire an employee. It doesn't have to be perfect; it just has to pass what we fancy lawyers call the smell test. If the reason does not smell fishy (and there is evidence supporting that reason), the employee can be fired. This is one of those tests, however, where the judge deciding a case will almost always use his or her own subjective meaning of good cause. If you get a judge who hates Evil Employers, good causes may be hard to come by. If you get one who thinks employers never, ever lie, then there are lots of good causes out there. What is the number one specific difference between good cause and just cause (meaning, what is likely not a "just cause" reason to fire someone)? The poor economic condition of the employer, or things that are not the employee's fault. If the company is not making money or has some kind of financial hardship (even a teeny, tiny one), the employer has good cause to fire an employee, but not just cause. But don't quote me. You might get an Evil Employer-loving judge.

The other thing that it is important to keep in mind about the freedom of at-will employment is the freedom to the employee that I mentioned earlier. While being a term employee may give you job security, it also protects your employer (and who wants to do that!). For instance, if you are a term employee and you quit, your employer may be able to sue you for breaking the agreement. Yikes! I blame English law and the harsh apprenticeship rules from which America modeled its present-day employment laws. I will give you a realistic example. After you quit your term job, your former employer may hire someone in a hurry, pay that person a higher salary, and then sue you to make you pay the difference between that person's salary and your previous one (and perhaps even any lost business attributed to your quitting your job). All of that could be considered your fault, and you would have to pay. The freedom granted to an employee in an at-will system may not be such a bad thing when you think about it.

I want to point out something right now. If you work for the Government (federal, State, or local) and not a private company, you may indeed already be in the just or good cause world. Government employees usually have some legal right to their job. You see, our federal Constitution (using the Bill of Rights and some additional amendments) protects our life, liberty, and property from being taken away by the Government unless they give you a chance to defend yourself first or very soon thereafter. In a typical Government employment case, this chance to defend yourself is usually called the ***grievance*** process. In a grievance, you have the right to challenge certain things your employer is trying to do to you (such as being fired), and make them stop. You are getting these things not because the Government loves you, or is being nice to you. The Government is doing it because it is the absolute minimum it has to do (Evil Government Employer!).

For you Government employees, I will spare you the detailed history lesson of how your right to a job is due to the Progressive Era in the early 20th century and the creation of a merit-based, professional civil service that led to laws being passed protecting you from being fired. It is enough to say that if you work for the Government, you probably are not an at-will employee. Keep in mind, however, that this is not always the case (you see, I still have to be lawyery at times, and speak in generalities).

If you don't work for the Government, how do you change your job from being employed at-will if you are already there? In theory, you simply ask. You negotiate. Free market scholars like to emphasize this. However, this type of agreement is usually reserved for very senior and experienced workers. In the real world, if most people ask this question, employers will look at them with narrowed eyes, assume they've read some book about employee rights where employers are considered evil, and peg them as troublemakers.

There is some hope, though. There are people out there who don't like employment at-will, and maybe even some employers. These people think they can fix the at-will system and make employees' lives better. Who is this great and powerful Oz-like being who loves employees? Surprise, it is the Government (when it is not acting as your employer). Remember when I said at the beginning that a law or an agreement may change at-will employment? Well, here come the legal changes.

Changes to Employment At-Will

Beyond individual employment contracts or union agreements, other things can change an employment agreement from the total, slightly scary freedom that is at-will employment. Obviously, the Government can pass laws and regulations that make it illegal for an employer to fire you in certain situations. For example, employment discrimination laws were passed making it unlawful to fire someone because of his or her race, religion, sex, disability, etc. Both federal and State laws do things like this as well, and they all have their own little quirks and pitfalls. We will talk about discrimination in Chapter 4.

However, it's not just legislatures that love to make changes and muck about with the free market. Courts do so as well. While a senator may write a law saying that an Evil Employer must do X, Y, and Z, judges cannot do that. When a judge looks at how an employer has treated an employee and thinks, "Hey! They can't fire a person that way. How can we fix this? Hmmm. Has a law been passed preventing this? No. Pfft, stupid politicians. Well then, we will have to assume ... uhh ... that ... I got it! I'll assume that the employment contract must have been changed unofficially but both the employer and employee somehow magically agreed!" Really.

How do courts do this? They look at what an employer either wrote or said to an employee over time. For example, one court ruled that if an employer told a secretary that she "had a job as long as she did good work," then that employee was not at-will anymore and could only be fired for good cause. Wow. Don't get too excited, though, because that is not how it is in most places. The point to remember is that an employer might say something to an employee or write something in an email that takes away the employer's ability to fire for no reason at all. Do not forget, though, that some States love at-will employment so much that nothing can change it except a clearly written agreement, perhaps even requiring the employee's own blood.

What else have courts done? Let's suppose that you were offered a job, moved your family to another State, bought a new house, and then, before your first day, you got fired. An employer can't do that, can they? That has got to be totally unfair, right? Hmm. Here I will have to trot out some legalese. This is sometimes called ***promissory estoppel***, and not all States accept it. Remember, if you are an at-will employee, an Evil Employer can fire you whenever it wants. So, if it can fire you after one hour on the job, why can't it fire you one hour before you start working? If the Evil Employer could do that, that would make sense in an at-will employment world, right? Yes.

However, some courts and judges think that even if this is okay, it should not be. To them, there is something fundamentally different from firing an employee who has actually worked for an employer, and dangling a job in front of an employee and firing them before they even get a chance to do any work. This is where the idea of promissory estoppel kicks in. If an employer offers an employee a job, and an employee relies on this job offer (such as turning down other jobs or moving to another place), this is now a promise (the promissory part) that the employer cannot take away (the estoppel part—the employer is prevented or stopped from changing its mind). If this promissory estoppel theory applies, then the employer is now required to give an employee a chance to prove that he or she can do the job. Sounds nice, doesn't it?

The larger question is how long the employer has to give you this chance. If we assume that an employer already wants to fire you, do you think you really have a future with this Evil Employer? Does a company have to wait one hour, one week, or one year before getting rid of you? This is where the law breaks down, because there is no simple answer. There are cases where a week is long enough, and cases where one year is too short. In general, however, the court simply looks to see if the employer gave you a fair chance at your job, and also takes into account what is happening to the employer (is it losing money, making money, growing, reorganizing, etc.). As you can see, the devil is in the details, and it is quite tricky. It is also something that rarely happens.

Sometimes, courts also treat *employment manuals* like contracts. If you are an employee, take a look at your company's manual. If you have a hardcopy, look at the inside cover or the first page. Do you see the lovely language saying that the manual is not a contract? Those words also suggest that only a fool would treat the manual as a contract, and you are not a fool. Also, note that the employer says it can change the manual whenever it wants. Why is that there? I blame New Jersey. In the mid-1980s, the New Jersey Supreme Court ruled that manuals were like contracts unless they had language like that. So all the manuals now do. You are probably wondering if that manual is a contract. You are going to love my answer: it depends. More precisely, it depends on what State you are in. In most places, but not all, the manual is not a contract, and an employer can change it or break it whenever it wants. The idea is that a manual is not meant to be binding; rather, it is meant to guide administrators and managers in a company and help them treat employees fairly. It would terrible if that was a contract and the employer actually had to obey its own rules.

Those are the usual ways in which courts sometimes change the basic rules surrounding employment at-will and give an employee some protection over being fired. Another common way gets its own special section, if only because most potential clients tend to ask me if it applies to them.

The Government Says You Can't Fire Me for What I Did, So There

Sometimes, an employee does something that is just so gosh-darned special that it would make a State cry if he or she got fired for it. So, the courts created the *tort* of **wrongful discharge** (also called wrongful termination or retaliatory discharge—I will describe what a "tort" is a bit later). The basic idea of wrongful discharge is that when the Government has an interest in something happening, it will not let an employer fire an employee for doing that "something". That "something" is referred to as a public policy. So, if it would be against the public policy of a State for an employee to get fired, the employee can't be fired. If the employee is fired, he or she can sue the employer to try and get their job back, and their lost wages, and sometimes even emotional harm and suffering.

I know that the concept of a public policy is not easy to understand, so let's start with an example—the classic case of jury duty. The Government says we need courts, and for our system of justice to work, we also need jurors to decide if laws have been broken. Now, suppose Evil Employer fires someone because they have to go on jury duty. In fact, let's suppose that all the Evil Employers in the State forbid their employees to serve on a jury. That would mean that all juries in the State would only be full of people without jobs. Well, reasons the State, even if employers can fire at-will employees whenever they want, we cannot let that happen in this case because it would not be fair and representative. So, instead, the State tells employers that they cannot interfere with a person's need to serve on a jury because jury duty is an important public policy that must be protected. If they do fire the employee, wrongful discharge comes into play.

That is just one example, though. What other kinds of things are protected, or more properly, what other public policies are protected? Well, this is where States frequently disagree but you can sort of group these public policies hidden in the law into four general categories: (1) refusing to commit a crime, (2) engaging in a right clearly guaranteed by a written law (for example, a law may require that a nurse report child abuse even if that child is related to the president of the hospital), (3) satisfying a public duty (for example, jury duty), and (4) whistle-blowing or complaining about something against the law. If the behavior that got you fired is in one of these areas, you might have been wrongfully fired. However, please keep in mind that there are grey areas in all of these categories, and you might think you are protected when you are not.

Now the Government Says You Can't Treat Me That Way, So Stop!

There is another, rare limit on what your employer can do to you at work. If an employer does something that is truly shocking, then it just might have committed the tort of ***intentional***

infliction of emotional distress. The reason this is rare is that the employer must truly do something that is extreme and outrageous, cannot be tolerated in our civilized society, and is beyond the bounds of all decency. In addition, the employer must actually cause you emotional or physical harm and intentionally mean to do it (or be so reckless that it knew it was likely you would get harmed). The reason this is so unusual is that, frankly, employers are rarely this bad (or courts rarely think what the employer did was extreme and outrageous).

Think of something really bad that an employer might do. Is it a kind of mental torture? Is it so incredibly cruel that it would be totally unacceptable to the average person? You should know this is not about fairness, or even morality. It is way beyond that.

With that said, some States actually demand a tiny bit less on the severity or outrageousness scale when dealing with employees and employers. They accept this lowering of the scale because there is a special relationship between employees and employers. Because employees rely on their employers so much for financial security, the law is a bit concerned about employers being evil and taking cruel advantage of employees. For example, one court found that it was outrageous that a company began firing people alphabetically until someone confessed to stealing from the company. Another example involved an employee who was strip-searched in front of a customer. Okay, the latter I think we can see is quite outrageous. But the first one? Some courts will say yes, but some courts will say no. My point in raising these two examples is that just because the law claims to demand incredible, crazy action by an employer, sometimes it can be a bit less outrageous than you think.

This is indeed a change to employment at-will, not in the sense that you can keep your job or anything. It is a change because you can hold your employer responsible for hurting you. It is important to remember that because of employment at-will, you can leave your job at any time. Yes, even before things get too outrageous and painful. You might think that if you do, you might miss the opportunity to have a better lawsuit. I always counsel my clients to do what is best for them and their families, and never go against that just to make a lawsuit better. It is a poor decision in life to choose to suffer more at work just to increase your chances of winning a lawsuit. Okay? I equally understand that, financially, many people feel like they have no choice but to stay in a painful job situation. If you are in that position, you see, you are already making the choice about what is best for you—staying in the job. That is fine.

In light of what I have just said, I would ask you this: is your employer really evil and treating you terribly, or do you just disagree with how they are treating you? If they are evil and being terrible, you just might have a claim against them.

What is a Tort?

I have used this word "tort" twice now, for both wrongful discharge and intentional infliction of emotional distress. It sounds like a fancy-pants legal word that you expect insufferable lawyers to use. Yep. A tort means nothing more than one person causing harm to another person. We call it a tort because (1) lawyers like to borrow French words sometimes just to annoy Latin scholars; (2) it's one letter shorter than the word "wrong", which is the English translation of the French word; and (3) if we use the word "tort" it sounds like we have super-expensive education and knowledge that you don't. There are certainly more explanations (more accurate ones too) that involve our American-English legal history.

So let me give you a tiny legal history lesson that just might explain what a tort is. When the United States of America became its own country, we borrowed a lot from English law. We did not borrow their statutes, or laws passed by the King, Queen, or Parliament. We hated them. We did borrow their common law. Common law was not really written down like statutes were. This law was gradually created out of the decisions made by judges and other legal officials over a thousand years. Think of it as judge-made law, as opposed to legislature-made law. That's not quite accurate, but it's a nice mental shortcut. Torts come out of the common law. They deal with harms that people cause others, and the attempt to make the person who caused the harm (or the tortfeasor) pay the victim for his or her actions. This is not criminal law—there is no punishment by the Government here. This is just between private people (and companies).

Judges do not like to think that they are making law when using common law. However, they do "find" new torts from time to time. Judges know they are not allowed to make law, so they engage in a little bit of lying—they simply claim to "find" a new way to explain what was already hidden in the common law. We typically call those "found" laws torts. It is certainly true that all torts flow from the idea that if you hurt someone by breaking society's rules (either on purpose or accidentally), you must pay for that harm. You could say that these torts are just a different way to explain how to analyze and calculate that harm in different situations.

You should be aware that common law torts are not laws passed by statute or by a legislature, and that courts *find* them sloshing around somewhere in the common law. Therefore, you may not find these laws in any written book of laws or legal *code*. You only learn them by reading case after case of law, and understanding the basic principles of each tort, including how a tort may change over time. At the same time, your State and local legislature does have the power to rewrite the common law and change it. It does that by passing a law, and now that law is written down and becomes a statute. When that happens, we call that *codifying* the common law. Now, with the common law reduced to a written statute, the courts follow the statute and its definition of the tort and not the common law's definition.

Sample Employment At-Will Consultation

Would you like to know what a consultation with a lawyer might be like? It might begin something like this.

Lawyer: So, I understand that you are having a problem at work.
Client: Yeah. I was fired.
Lawyer: That's a big problem all right. Did you have a contract with your employer?
Client: Yeah.

Lawyer: You did?

Client: Of course. That first day, you know, they gave me all kinds of forms to sign, about financial stuff, manuals, you know.

Lawyer: Oh, yes. There is a lot of that isn't there? But did your employer ever tell you about how long you could work there, or anything like that?

Client: Well, no. They did give me an offer letter. I have it here.

(Lawyer reads the letter, and notes that it's standard in that the employee is told the name of his position, his salary, and his start date. Nothing that would take it out of at-will employment. A good lawyer would do well to explain at-will employment law at this time, so the client will have an idea of where the questions will be going and why).

Lawyer: So, why do you think you were fired?

Client: I don't know. That's why I'm here.

(Apparently, Client does not trust lawyers. A common assumption, if misplaced).

Lawyer: Okay. Did your employer tell you why you were fired?

Client: Yes.

Lawyer: And what was their reason?

Client: They said that I was not getting along with other employees. But that isn't true. I get along with everyone.

Lawyer: Why do you think they would say that?

Client: I don't know. I think they wanted to get rid of me.

Lawyer: Oh? And why is that?

Client: I don't really know. I think it might be because I kept seeing all the mistakes my co-workers were making. I told my supervisor, and then he told everyone else. Then everyone started making fun of me, and I told them to leave me alone and mind their own business.

(Note that once the Client starts talking, he or she actually does have an idea about why he or she was fired. Sometimes, it takes time for people to get comfortable talking with a lawyer. We understand, and try to get people talking in general so they eventually open up).

Lawyer: What kinds of mistakes did you complain about?

(In asking this question, the lawyer is trying to determine if this is a usual, "employee disagrees with employee" moment, or perhaps it might be a complaint that is protected by a whistleblower law).

Client: I just saw them wasting time, when I was working so hard. I tried to be the best employee I could, and resented when other people were taking advantage of their job.

(In the perverse world of the law, I am sorry to say that this noble sentiment rarely gets any kind of legal protection).

Lawyer: I see.

(Translation: rats! Nothing there).

Client: I know. It's really unfair isn't it?
Lawyer: Absolutely. I am sorry.

CHAPTER 2

WHEN YOUR EMPLOYER LIES ABOUT YOU (DEFAMATION)

What is Defamation?

You just lost your job. You feel angry and terrible. The next day, you get a phone call from a friend of yours who still works with your former employer. He tells you that the company sent out an e-mail saying you were fired because you stole lots of money from them (which is not true). Anger does not even begin to describe how you feel. Can an employer really do this?

This is what defamation is all about, and it stings. Defamation is when someone (or some Evil Employer) tells other people false things about you, and those false things impact your reputation. How do you know if you were defamed? Well, you would need to have evidence of these (overly) simplified things: an employer (1) wrote or spoke (2) a false fact about you (3) to someone else (this cannot be you) (4) either knowing that the fact was false or should have known it was false, and (5) you were harmed by the words.

Many employees come to see me with worries about defamation. Sometimes it is because they were accused of doing something they deny doing. For example suppose a secretary was fired. The company accused her of stealing. That sounds really bad, doesn't it? Surely if she stole, then she was properly fired. Then more facts come out. She was just entering payroll into the computer. She made a few mistakes. Her supervisor did not catch the mistakes, and people got paid too much, including her. When the company found out, they accused her of doing it on purpose. They also called the police. Guess what? More and more companies are doing things like this.

The Employer Has to Communicate the False Fact to Someone Else

But is that example above defamation? No, not yet. You see, to be defamation, the employer actually has to *publish* or share the false information to someone besides the employee. In the example about the secretary above, up to one point, the company had not told anyone but her. That's not true, you say? Other people in the company must have talked about her and about her alleged theft? Of course. We can assume that people in the company discussed the secretary's actions and whether the employer should or should not fire her. Courts have decided that employers, in order to conduct business, have to let their employees talk in many situations, and that this cannot be considered defamation. Therefore, if the company tells only those employees who need to know about things (like people in human resources, for example), then that does not count as defamation.

Okay, you might say, as you scratch your head. What if the company tells everyone in the company, say, by email, that she was fired for stealing? If this happens, the company *might* be in trouble. Certain States have decided that employers should be able to tell their employees almost everything, and should not be sued for defamation. Other States are a bit more sensitive to such statements and only permit those employees who need to know in order to do their jobs to be told (for example, human resources personnel, the employee's supervisor, other executives in the chain of command, etc). In the end, if an employer has a good reason for telling other employees (such as for company morale or to stop future acts that are similar), there is likely no defamation. Lawyers and courts sometimes call this idea of protecting employers and employees from defamation "intra-corporate immunity".

Fine! Sheesh, what a crazy law, and we haven't even gotten to whether it was false or not. I know. One more thing. The employer in this example called the police. We want people to call the police when they think a crime has been committed, don't we? If people could get sued for defamation by calling the police, what would happen? People would not call the police, real crimes would not be reported, and the world would be a more dangerous place. So, in order to prevent this, States and courts generally try to protect people who call the police from defamation as well. This is another type of immunity or freedom from being sued for defamation.

Similarly, if the employer must share information with other agencies of the Government besides the police, this can be protected as well. Usually, this might occur if the employee wants unemployment, or files a claim of discrimination, or says that the employer broke a law. The employer is allowed to share information in order to defend or explain itself. There are a few other forms of protection against defamation, but these are likely the main types that you will find in an everyday employment context.

Just to make sure that no rule is always set in stone, and to further confuse everyone, you know these types of immunity or protections from defamation? Guess what? An employer can lose that protection if it behaves in a really, really bad way. What would qualify as bad? You are going to hate me. It depends, again, on the State where you live. Usually, a State will require some kind of bad motivation on the part of the employer, or evidence that the employer wanted to hurt the employee, before it will lose its protection. The truth is, there are so many possibilities here, and States are all over the map, that I really cannot be more clear. Just know that an employer can sometimes lose its protection. Got a headache yet? I hope not.

Let's turn back to our example now. Let's assume that this employer did tell someone who was not protected. When this secretary applied for a job with another company, Evil Employer told them that she was fired for stealing. This is the classic case of defamation in the employment context. Some of you might be thinking, but, isn't that true? Didn't the company fire her because she stole? No. They fired her because they *thought* she stole, and that is the important difference. This is where defamation happens in employment. When a company gets sloppy and tells other people, typically future employers, about why someone was fired, they can get in trouble. If the company tells others outside of the business, or even suggests, that an employee did in fact do something wrong, that can be defamation *if the employee can prove he or she is innocent*.

You Have to Prove It's False

All right. We finally get to the false part of defamation law. You think you might even be an expert on this because of all those lawyer and courtroom TV shows you've watched. Those can be fun and entertaining. Everyone knows that, in defamation cases, truth is a total defense, right? Wrong, but only in the strict legal sense. You see, when someone thinks they have been defamed, they actually have to *prove* that the statement about them is false or a lie. So, truth is not really something the employer has to prove as a defense to defamation. Falsehood is something the employee has to prove. In the end, it means the same thing for most people. It is not up to lawyers and courts, though. I will not bore you by explaining burdens of proof and what happens when the evidence is in that fanciest of fancy terms, *equipoise* (it means a tie).

In the example I gave, the secretary would have to prove that she did not steal the money in order to have a case of defamation against her employer. In other words, she would have to prove that it was an accident (or that she did not actually do it), and that she did not give herself more money on purpose. In the absence of clear evidence proving otherwise, you can see that a lot depends on whether other people believe the employee or not.

Opinions and Free Speech

Not all lies are really lies, and not all false statements can be defamation. You see, in general, the First Amendment protects our right to free speech at least against the Government. This does not mean that private employers can lie about you and there is nothing you can do. But it does mean that courts (who are part of the Government and thus bound to obey the First Amendment) cannot make it unlawful for people to express opinions that you don't like or don't want them to say. In general, that is.

An opinion is not a false fact that can support a defamation claim. To be sure, some opinions can contain false statements, but it is complicated to tease those apart. For the purposes of this book and your information, you should just know that opinions are not facts. Opinions generally cannot be proven either false or true, while facts can be. If you want to know if you have a case against your employer, you will want to focus on what the employer is saying about you factually.

Examples? Suppose Evil Employer tells Future Super Nice Employer that you were fired when in fact you resigned or quit (as an aside, employers frequently give employees this choice, either quit or be fired. Not much of a choice, is it?). If you can prove that you quit but your former employer claimed that you were fired, then the employer has just "published a false fact" about you. That can be defamation (it isn't defamation yet though, as you will read below).

Let's get into a greyer area, shall we? Let's suppose that your former employer gives its evil eye to employee (plaintiff) lawyers and adopts the Thumper rule. Remember Thumper from *Bambi*? If you don't have anything nice to say, don't say anything at all? If your employer says nothing about you but just confirms your employment, and will not give any other information, is this spreading a false fact about you? Is this suggesting that you did something wrong? Almost all the time, no, this is not defamation. However, some courts have found that employers who use the Thumper rule must actually follow it. If they sometimes release positive information, then the failure to speak positively in favor of an employee can be interpreted as a negative. There is more to this small point (as you might guess), but I wanted to let you know that, in general, this is not defamation unless additional facts suggest otherwise.

Can You Prove You Have Been Harmed?

Let's suppose that you can prove that an employer lied about you. Does that mean you win? You would think so, wouldn't you? But no, lies and falsehoods are something we have to accept in life. Defamation only kicks in for those lies that actually hurt you in some way, and you can prove it.

So far, I have refrained from calculating how you have been harmed, and putting a price tag on it, and things like that. It is a crude business, and does not really lend itself to a book. However, defamation law is a bit different in my opinion. In order to take a situation where someone has been spreading false facts about you and turn it into a defamation case, you need to show that you have been harmed. This can be difficult.

You see, judges are very busy people. They don't want to hear 'he said that', and 'she said that', and have to make a decision. Judges want people to grow up and solve their own problems. Unless.

Unless you can prove that not only someone lied about you, but that you were harmed by it.

How do you prove things like this? Of course, anyone can have evidence of harm by simply saying how much it hurt their feelings that someone falsely accused him or her of doing unnatural things with chickens (yes, I use this example in my class). How much is that worth? Well, to the cold, cruel law, it's up to the judge or jury to measure your pain, embarrassment, or suffering. Have you been harmed to the tune of $1, $100, $1,000, or $100,000? Judges and juries can be awfully tolerant of your pain, or think it's not so bad and you are just wasting their time.

In the employment world though, it can be easier to show harm. If the employer lied about you, and you lost your job, you can now say you have been harmed because you lost the wages and salary of that job. You see, if someone lies about your love of chickens, it's hard to say how much that is worth. If, however, you lose a job or job offer, it becomes easier and much clearer to put a dollar amount on that pain (Company X was going to hire you for $100,000 until they talked to Evil Former Employer and then they decided not to hire you—you have been harmed because you lost that new job if Evil Former Employer lied about you).

You know what? Employers know this too. Now, most employers do not give detailed references anymore, but instead only tell others when you worked for them, and what your job title was. They blame lawyers for this. In turn, lawyers blame sloppy employers for lying and not keeping their mouths closed. I am certainly biased, but I think lawyers have the better of this argument.

In addition, there are some kinds of lies or false facts that are so bad, the law will assume that you have been damaged and hurt. This is usually called defamation *per se*. What kinds of things are as bad as this? If the employer makes a statement suggesting you committed a serious crime, have a contagious disease, are unfit to do your job, or injures your business reputation, then they are in trouble. In most States, defamation *per se* means that the law assumes you have been damaged, and you do not have to introduce detailed evidence of how you have been harmed. In an actual lawsuit, of course you still would introduce as much evidence as possible. But defamation *per se* gets Evil Employers all nervous and sweaty when it happens.

In our example, the employer may have committed defamation *per se* because it told the other company the secretary was fired because she stole. Stealing is a serious crime that satisfies this special standard.

Evil Employer Intent

Okay, so, let's assume the Evil Employer has spread false facts about you to others, and you have been harmed. This is still not quite enough (but you are nearly there). Defamation claims require that the employer have an evil motive, either on purpose or by being carelessly reckless. In defamation law, this is called ***malice***. An employer will not be held responsible unless an employee can show that the employer spread the facts either knowing that they were false or lacking sufficient reason for believing the statements were true. In other words, if the employer does not care whether what it says is false (this is intentionally spreading false information), or if it spreads information while knowing there is some real doubt about whether something is false or misleading (this is recklessly spreading false information), then you likely have a defamation claim.

But. There is always a but. Employers do have defenses to defamation claims. There are many of them, and they depend on different facts; indeed, entire books can be written just on those defenses. I daresay that many a defense firm has done so. For our purposes, I have just tried to lay out the *simplest* way to find out if defamation has occurred.

Interfering With Your Attempt to Find a New Job

It's true, as I just wrote, that a former employer defames an employee if it spreads lies about the employee. Sometimes, however, defamation is just too hard to prove. Further, crafty employers will try to get around this and still cause an employee trouble. What can an employee do? Increasingly, lawyers are using another legal theory called ***intentional interference with a business expectancy***. With a name like that, you know it's another tort. I will say at the outset that this idea is still being fleshed out in the courts right now, so the law is not so clear.

To understand the basics, let's begin with an example. Let's suppose that Evil Employer fires Perfect Employee. Perfect Employee applies for a job with Good Employer. Good Employer contacts Evil Employer to confirm that Perfect Employee was, well, perfect. We know that if Evil Employer lies, this can be defamation. Suppose instead of lying, Evil Employer simply says that it will neither admit nor deny that Perfect Employee worked there. Good Employer hears this information and refuses to hire the Perfect Employee. This stinks, but is it illegal?

To prove that an employer unlawfully interfered with someone's future at-will employment, an employee will usually have to prove about five things: (1) a future job offer had been made or was about to be made, (2) the former employer knew about that job offer, (3) the former employer intentionally interfered with this hiring process, (4) (this step only applies if the future job is an at-will position) the former employer used *improper* methods of some kind, and (5) the employee did not get the job because of the former employer's actions.

I know that the phrase 'business expectancy' can seem a little strange, but that is because this tort applies to all sorts of things beyond future employment. I am keeping things simple and addressing only a very common use here. With that in mind, if an employee has proof that a future employer wants to hire him, then this is enough. Next an employee would have to prove that the former employer knew about this job prospect. Typically, this is established when the future employer gives the old one a call and asks for information. Step five is proven as soon as you don't get the job.

Steps three and four are the tricky ones. An at-will employee needs to show that an employer *intentionally* interfered here, and in doing so, used *improper* methods. So, an employer really has to be evil and actually try to prevent you from getting a new job? Yes, but that's not the only situation that can satisfy this *intent* step. If the employer was certain that a person would not get a job by its actions, or that it was very likely that a person would not get a job, then an employee has enough evidence of intentional action. Let's use our example. By withholding information, Evil Employer should be aware that it is very likely that Perfect Employee will not get the job. We do not know if Evil Employer is actually trying to prevent the employee from getting hired, but we know that it is very likely to end in that result.

But what about improper methods? What are those? This is one part of the tort where the law is a little grey. Here is a list of what some courts have found improper: defamation, violating another law, committing a crime, committing another civil wrong or tort, engaging in violence or threats of violence, bribery, fraud, misrepresentation, misuse of confidential information, unfair competition, duress or undue influence, and violating an industry standard or ethical rule. Just with this list you can probably guess that the law is still being formed. In developing this legal theory, courts tend to look at what a former employer said or did and whether the employer had any decent reason for its behavior.

Back to our example, though, has Evil Employer used improper methods? Hmm. It is possible to argue that Evil Employer is failing to follow the industry standard of confirming basic employment facts. It is also a good argument that the former employer has no real reason to deny this information to anyone—it has nothing to protect by withholding the information. Accordingly, I think we can say the employer has probably committed this tort.

Probably?! Can't you even give a straight answer about your own darn example!? Sorry, but I told you the law is developing here, and there are grey areas. What just might be unlawful today can be lawful tomorrow and vice versa. What I am trying to do is give you enough information so that you can gauge whether or not your former employer just might be doing something wrong.

Oh. To confuse you further, this tort can also apply to current contracts too. For example, if you have a job and a former employer gets you fired, you apply this legal theory to see if you can hold them responsible. The only difference is in step one —you just have to prove you had a valid employment contract (at-will or otherwise). Okay?

Chapter 3

Johnny Be Good: Non-Competition Agreements

The law is a wonderful thing. We like to think we are free, and that combining our knowledge and skill with our effort, we can have a pretty nice life. Pretty much the American Dream, right? Hah. Wake up from that dream! No one ever said you had a *right* to a nice life. Even our Declaration of Independence only talks about a *pursuit* of happiness—thus, there is no right to happiness, I am afraid. Just like the Government takes away part of your labor in the form of taxes, your employer can take away some of your labor too (your ability to work for a competing company), if you let it.

But what about all your knowledge, skill, and effort? How can an employer take those things from you? This is America, right? Well, who ever said you could not give those things away? Remember, we start out free, with employment at-will, and a broad horizon of hope and choice in front of us. Then we begin to live in the real world, and we make decisions. Sometimes, we choose to work for someone we think is a good, kind, and caring employer. This good, kind, caring employer seduces you with talk about how fantastic you are, how lucky they are to have you, and then they ask you to sign something that says you agree not to work for those other Evil Employers out there. After all, who would want to work for those Evil ones? You are, of course, besotted with your employer and you sign the paper. Uh oh.

You have just signed something called a non-competition agreement. You have just given up the freedom to quit your job, take your body (and your experience, education, knowledge, and skills), and go work for a competing business. Oops. It's true you can still quit and walk away from that job, but you may have just agreed not to work for anyone else in the area for a while. So, all that knowledge, skill, and training you have, you cannot use (at least not easily). And no, the employer does not have to pay you at all while you are not working (well, unemployment might apply, but that is different).

Back in the day, non-competition agreements were usually reserved for high-level corporate executives (usually with titles that began with "Vice President of"). Evil Employers realized that, hey, if we can use them against the rich and powerful, then we can surely use them against "lowly" regular employees too. Today, sales people sign them, hair stylists do, auto mechanics do, and on and on. I am sorry to say that non-competition agreements are everywhere now.

It should be clear that non-competition agreements are not nice things for employees. Courts usually agree with this sentiment as well, and they are usually quite hostile to them. In technical terms, non-competition agreements are called restraints on trade, and courts don't like those. They do of course recognize the theory behind having them—giving the employer a limit on an employee's ability to work for competitors allows the employer to train an employee and provide him or her with super special secrets so that the employee becomes Super Intelligent Efficient Employee (whether or not this actually happens does not matter to lovers of the theory). Just because courts do not like these agreements does not mean that they will simply ignore them because you want them to do so. You need to help a court by giving them a good reason to ignore a non-competition agreement or otherwise find them unenforceable (usually, this involves arguing that what the employer is trying to protect in such an agreement is not reasonable compared to the restriction it is putting on the employee's ability to work).

What are some good reasons then? Well, first things first. The actual State in which you live and work is incredibly important here. In some States, non-competition agreements are viewed as such a bad thing, that they are almost impossible to enforce (hello, California) and laws are passed restricting their use. With the caveat in mind that individual States love to tinker with this issue, in general, you will probably want to read the agreement and look for three general things: (1) what are you actually prohibited from doing (the work limit), (2) where are you prevented from working (the geographical limit), and (3) how long are you prevented from doing it (the time limit). There are no easy answers here. Courts need to look at each employer and the work it does, what training or information it has given you, the type of work you did for the employer, and then compare that to the restrictions in the agreement. If that is not enough, courts will often flip back and forth on the right way to interpret these things over the years, so that a non-competition agreement that is valid in one year is not in the next, and vice versa.

To help you understand things a bit, let's take a look at a very simple non-competition clause. An agreement might look like this: *"Upon the Employee leaving the employ of Evil Employer for any reason at all, Employee agrees that he or she will not work for any competitor of Evil Employer within a 50 mile radius for a period of 2 years."* You should see right away that this agreement applies to an employee who is not only fired, but one who quits as well. This means that, if this agreement is valid, and if your employer is a huge, evil jerk and you want to leave, you cannot work for a competitor for two years. Ouch.

However, this sample agreement may fail what is called the "janitor case". If a non-competition clause provides that you cannot work in any way for a competitor, then that agreement as written may not be valid. For example, if you worked as a computer operator for Evil Employer, and under Evil Employer's non-competition agreement you cannot even work as a janitor for Good Employer, then a court may say that the agreement is not valid, at least as written. Why? Because the employer has no good reason to prevent you from working as a janitor—the employer did not give you any super special secrets in custodial engineering, so you should not be prevented from doing that. If an employer tries to do so, then it is being unreasonable. At the same time, if the employer only tries to stop you from working as a computer operator for Good Employer (who will, of course, become evil later), a court is likely to agree with

Evil Employer and enforce this agreement against you. Of course, many courts will simply agree to rewrite the non-competition agreement to fix this problem, but not all of them do.

Suppose an Evil Employer tries to prevent you from working for any competitor anywhere on Earth, not just 50 miles from where you worked? Is that okay? You think I am going to tell you of course not, that's crazy. I cannot, because the answer depends on too many questions. Ugh, you say, you are just trying to get me to pay some lawyer friend of yours for an opinion. First of all, I have no lawyer friends—I only have competitors! Second, if a company has an honest worldwide reach, then such worldwide prohibition can actually be reasonable. However, it is much more likely that an employer will specify some amount of miles around where the employee worked.

You might well be asking, what about that 50 miles, is that okay? Unfortunately, I have to give you the same answer—maybe. The shorter that range, the more likely it will be valid. Why? Because you can always commute short term or make a modest move for a new employer. This is not a great solution to your problem, I know. But then, you signed the agreement (whether or not you had a meaningful choice is a different question). For what it is worth, courts commonly uphold ranges of 25 to 50 miles as a reasonable limit. Not always, so don't quote me.

Okay fine, we have the work limit and range down, so let's talk about the real whammy, the time limit. How long do you have to sit on your thumbs? Most non-competition agreements provide that you cannot work for about 1 to 2 years. Absent unusual circumstances, that kind of time restriction is usually valid. Kapow.

This does not mean that you face imminent bankruptcy. Usually, non-competition agreements only apply if you work for a competitor of your former employer. So that means ... wait. In most jobs, while working, you develop at least experience if not skills that help you in the specific job you do. That specific job experience is likely only valuable to whom? Oh yeah, probably businesses in the same field as your current employer. In other words, it's likely that the future Good Employers who want to hire you are competitors of the Evil Employer. Nonetheless, there are potential employers out there.

If you have signed a non-competition agreement, you are probably beginning to panic, and scream about how evil the Evil Employer really is. Yep. If I believed that employers actually paid their employees a fair amount of money to buy this restriction, I could like non-competes. I don't believe it though. This is why I hate them. I also hate the fact that most employees do not have enough power to refuse to sign them and still keep their jobs. Most employees are therefore given a choice: work for me and get paid but promise to not work in the same area, or get fired (or not hired). This is indeed freedom of contract. This does not give me warm fuzzies about such freedom though.

So what can you do if you signed one and want to get out of it? First, definitely go see a lawyer. What can we do? We start by looking at the agreement to see if we can find a way to argue that the agreement is not valid. We don't stop there. We then ask you to tell us about any skeletons in the closet of Evil Employer. The skeletons we look for are other laws that the company might be breaking. With this information, we then try to get the employer to release you from the agreement. If you leave on good terms with your employer, this can be easier. If you leave on bad terms, they will usually need some pressure to release you. The pressure comes from those legal skeletons. So, pay attention at work, okay?

CHAPTER 4

DISCRIMINATION

What is Discrimination?

Welcome to the section on the super-duper-number-one-oh-yeah-I-am-going-to-sue-you most popular exception to employment at-will—discrimination. I am sure you have read about, or seen some movie or TV show about, illegal discrimination. Let's start by defining it. At its simplest level, discrimination means that your employer is treating you differently because you are a member of a legally protected group of people.

Really? That's it? Yep. We even have a fancy name for it—*individual disparate treatment*. I will call it individual discrimination for ease of reference. Individual discrimination cases focus on a single employee at a time. This distinguishes it from class action cases (systemic disparate treatment and systemic disparate impact). An employee may have a valid case of individual discrimination if he or she can prove three things: (1) membership in a protected class, (2) the employer did something bad to him or her, and (3) the reason the employer did something bad is because he or she is a member of that protected class.

Not All Discrimination Breaks the Law

Well, let's start off with number one. You need to belong to a legally protected group. What kinds of people are protected? Are you? I can say without knowing you that, yes, you are already in a protected class. Really? Yep. No way? Trust me. How is that possible? Weren't these types of laws meant to protect minorities? That's a funny one. You see, our anti-discrimination laws generally don't identify the minority group they were meant to protect, only the group itself. For example, a law might say that it is illegal to discriminate against someone because of his or her race. What race is protected? All of them. Why? Because even if our anti-discrimination laws might have been meant to protect only a select group or minority race, that selective protection never made it into the law. The Supreme Court of the United States has said, in no uncertain terms, that employment discrimination laws protect against the "majority" discriminating against the "minority", the "minority" discriminating against the "majority" (so-called reverse discrimination), and heck, while we are at it, even majority vs. majority (another kind of reverse discrimination), and minority vs. minority discrimination is illegal too. Whoa. That's a lot of discrimination.

Let me explain, and let's stick with race as our protected group for this discussion. Some people think that discrimination only occurs when Caucasians discriminate against African-Americans. That is wrong. The only thing the law cares about is whether the reason the employer did a bad thing to an employee was his or her race, whether that race is African-American, Caucasian, Jewish (yes, it's legally a race) or whatever other race it may be. This means that if an African-American mistreats an African-American for racial reasons, that is discrimination. Same thing if an African-American mistreats a white person or Caucasian.

Race, however, is not the only protected group; it was just my beginning example. The main classes of people protected are based on: ***race, color*** (yes, color, the federal law was passed in 1964 after all)***, religion, national origin, sex, pregnancy, disability, age*** (only 40 years or older), and to a lesser but different extent, ***whistleblowers*** (or employees who have complained about the company breaking a law). At this time, there is no national law preventing discrimination based on someone's sexual preference, although many States do have such laws (but hang on until we talk about stereotyping).

So, when looking at these protected classes, both women and men are protected. Yep. African-Americans, blacks, Native Americans, Aleuts, Hispanics, Muslims, Christians? Mmmhmm. And all people over 40 too, right? Ahem. Not so fast. It is true that it is illegal to discriminate against people 40 years of age or older in employment. However, remember that whole minority vs. majority, or reverse discrimination thing I just wrote? It appears the Supreme Court thinks that does not apply to age discrimination cases. In other words, it is discrimination only when something happens to *older* employees, not younger ones. In a line from the Supreme Court explaining its point of view, the enemy of people 40 years of age is not someone who is 50, but someone who is 30. Thus, it appears that the only kind of age discrimination that is illegal is harming older, not younger, people. So if you are 45 and the employer gives the 55 year-old employee something you do not get, that is not unlawful age discrimination.

Are you still with me? Because we are about to get more complicated. Remember how I mentioned stereotypes before? For our purposes, a ***stereotype*** is some trait or characteristic that our society assumes that a group or a bunch of people have. It can be a positive stereotype or a negative one. When I teach, the first day we talk about common stereotypes. It can make students uncomfortable, and they are understandably usually nervous about offering them up. Let me give you a couple negative ones (prepare to get insulted and annoyed): African-Americans are angry, Jewish people are cheap, White people are ignorant, Muslims are violent, the mentally ill are dangerous, women are too sensitive, men are clueless, Christians are stupid, old people are slow, etc.

Of course, a stereotype or an assumption can absolutely be false, and it can certainly not apply to an individual employee. If an employer treats an employee based on a stereotype, that can be discrimination too. The classic case involves gender stereotypes. Once upon a time in a case before the Supreme Court, a woman was up for promotion. Despite being very successful and making the company lots of money, she did not get the promotion. In order to get the job, she was told she needed to dress more like a woman, wear makeup, and go to charm school (no, I am not making this up). You see, the Evil Employer thought that the female employee was not acting enough like the stereotypical woman, or how it thought a woman should behave. This stereotyping was enough to be discrimination.

So remember, an employer cannot do something bad to you (1) because you belong to a protected category, or (2) because of a stereotype based on the protected group to which you belong.

Bad Things Happen

I am going to say something that will shock you. You see, we like to think that discrimination is bad. We know that we have anti-discrimination laws, so all discrimination must be illegal, right? Wrong. Believe it or not, the law allows some discrimination, even discrimination based on protected reasons. Consider this example. Suppose an Evil Employer decides to spend money on some new desks. It buys ten of them. Suppose there are eleven employees, and only one is a woman. Suppose Evil Employer thinks men are better workers just because they are so manly, and the men get the new desks. We agree that the reason the female employee did not get the desk is because of her sex, right? Is this discrimination? Yes. Is this illegal discrimination? Generally, no. Shocked?

You are losing even more faith in our legal system, aren't you? Well, the reason courts may permit this kind of discrimination is that they, well, read the actual anti-discrimination law. In employment, the typical law will say something like this: "it is an unlawful employment practice for an employer to discriminate against any employee with respect to the terms, conditions, and privileges of employment because of such employee's sex [feel free to insert a different category here]." So, courts have ruled, as a matter of logic, not all discrimination has been made illegal—only discrimination that affects terms, conditions, and privileges of employment.

Does not getting a new desk affect those things? Courts have said no. They created a lovely little phrase to define what types of bad things do affect the terms, conditions, and privileges of employment: ***an adverse employment action***. Only adverse employment actions or harmful employment decisions that discriminate are illegal. So, is not getting a desk harmful enough? No. Usually. Almost always.

So what are these bad things? It's time for a list: ***not getting hired, being fired, not getting a promotion, getting paid less, getting a demotion, or a reduction in work hours***. This is in no way a complete list, but these are the most common types of adverse employment actions or *bad things*. If your employer has done one of these things to you (or something very similar) in a discriminatory way, you have been hurt enough to make a claim of discrimination.

Are you ready for a typical bit of legal fuzziness? I am about to take back what I just said (at least a little bit). The United States Supreme Court has never actually ruled that you need an adverse employment action in an employment discrimination case. Meaning that if you have very clear proof (like a confession) that an employer gave an employee an old desk just because she was a woman, that still might be discrimination. Why? Because courts treat cases differently when they involve extremely obvious or ***direct evidence*** of discrimination (e.g., "I am putting your desk near the bathroom because you are black"). Historically, this whole "adverse employment action" requirement was created by courts in cases where employees did not have direct or clear evidence of discrimination, but only indirect or circumstantial evidence. *What is direct evidence?* In discrimination law, direct evidence is something that, all by itself, shows that the employer treated the employee differently because of a protected reason. The simplest way to describe this type of evidence is to think of a confession—the employer admits that it did something to an employee because of his or her race, sex, age, or some other protected group or reason.

If something is not direct evidence (e.g., there is no confession), then it is circumstantial evidence. **Circumstantial evidence** is anything and everything that suggests discrimination took place, but it is not clear all by itself that discrimination occurred—the circumstances suggest discrimination, but there is not any clear evidence of discrimination. For example, these things can be circumstantial evidence of discrimination: a manager calls an African-American man "boy" (this shows that the employer is thinking about the person's race); a female employee is told she is acting like a bitch (only females are called that derogatory term); an older employee is told that he or she lacks the skills of the modern workplace (this suggests the stereotype that old dogs cannot learn new tricks); and so forth.

Anything can be circumstantial evidence of discrimination, which is why cases can be so complex. There may be innocent explanations for any kind of circumstantial evidence, but this kind of evidence can certainly suggest discrimination too.

When employees only have circumstantial evidence of discrimination (and, overwhelmingly, this is what most employees have), the courts are a bit more kind or lenient to employers. In these cases, courts tend to demand that the employee present some kind of adverse employment action. Why? Because it helps to show that something important is going on rather than just an employee who is unhappy about how he or she is being treated.

As I write this, I can sense your confusion and frustration. Direct and circumstantial evidence? Adverse employment actions or bad things? How do I make sense of this? This is precisely why this area of the law is so complex. The best advice I can give you is this: if you have direct or clear evidence of discrimination, you probably do not need to show that your employer hurt you very much—the evidence alone is highly offensive. However, if you do not have direct evidence but only circumstantial evidence, then you will probably need an adverse employment action. This short summary will guide you correctly in almost all cases of employment discrimination.

Proving that the Bad Thing Happened Because of a Protected Reason

Okay. Here is the hardest thing to prove, and it is really hard. An employee needs to show that the reason the bad employment decision was made by the employer is specifically because of the employee's membership in a protected class. Let me use an example to make it easier: a female employee would need to show that she got fired because she is a woman.

How can you do that? Did I mention this is hard? The employer sometimes, but rarely, actually confesses: "I am sorry, Julia, but we need to let you go because only a man can do this job well." If this happens, you have direct evidence and therefore a strong case right? Yes, well, maybe. In theory.

I do not live in a world of theory. If a client tells me something like that happened, do I leap out of my chair and say, "Let's go get those bastards!"? Nope. I ask if there was anyone else around when this confession occurred. Odds are, if there was a confession, it was made in a one-on-one private meeting. I fully expect the Evil Employer and its minions to claim that this confession never, ever happened. If the only proof of discrimination is this confession, unfortunately, you will likely not have enough evidence to prove discrimination.

How can this be? This is a confession! You see, lawyers expect people to lie. Judges were once lawyers, and expect the same thing. The judge also knows that the employee has every reason to lie in these one-on-one conversations if this alone could prove a case of discrimination. In the back of his or her mind, the judge knows the employer has a reason to lie too, but since the employee has to prove discrimination, the judge does not worry about this. Most judges will therefore not permit an employment discrimination case to go forward if the only evidence of discrimination is a one-on-one confession that the employer does not admit happened. A one-on-one confession therefore is not likely to be enough proof.

What else do you need? Let's stick with the confession thing for a bit. If there was another person in the room who admits the confession took place, that helps. If perhaps another employee happened to overhear the confession, that's good too. To a lesser extent, if the employee leaves the one-on-one meeting and quickly proceeds to complain to another worker and mentions the confession, that can help as well.

Do you see what we are doing? We are trying to see what information is out there that suggests discrimination took place.

Like I wrote, confessions rarely happen. The usual discrimination case therefore looks for other things (as I wrote in the last section, these other things are called circumstantial evidence). Unfortunately, I cannot give you a list of all the types of evidence that may or may not exist to help prove a case. Courts keep creating unique tests of how to prove a case of employment discrimination based on certain facts (they have a different one if an employee is fired, or demoted, or laid off, etc.). Trust me, if I went into that deep, dark legal jungle, neither of us would come out of it sane (we call that law school).

Let's instead focus on the typical information that you, the employee, might actually have right now. On this quick information gathering train, we have two stops: people and paper. When trying to know what information people have, first look inside your own head and ask this question: "why do I think Evil Employer is doing this bad thing to me because of {insert reason}." For now, let's keep using "because of sex" as the reason. If your answer is that you don't know, then you are unlikely to have much proof that discrimination occurred.

In my experience, your instincts help you know when discrimination is occurring, but instincts are not proof. However, your instinct was likely triggered by a whole host of things happening to you that you probably never really focused on before. You need to tap into that internal list of things. Try to remember when something was said to you, what was actually said, who said it, and who was around who might have overheard it. You want to try to remember as much detail as possible.

You may even want to write it down to guard against forgetting things. Your memory may not be perfect, but I guarantee you that as time goes on, if you do not write things down, you will only forget more. So, write them down. You should know, however, that if you do, if there is a lawsuit in your future, Evil Employer just might get access to these notes. Be careful.

If you choose to write things down, you can make them read like a detective novel. You can also just jot down random thoughts or notes. You can order them according to when they happened. It does not matter now, just put them down how you want. Again, you want to try to write down as much detail as possible. If you know the date, great. If not, do you know the month, or the season, or was it before Christmas but after Thanksgiving? Do you remember who said it, who was around when it was said, or who you talked to about it?

It might not look like much when you write down "my supervisor told me that I never do anything right." However, it just might be that you have lots of such facts, and then you might remember your supervisor saying "you are such a woman" at another time. Is your supervisor discriminating against you because of your sex? Logically, you might be able to connect the dots between the memories of your supervisor not liking you to the statement that you act like such a woman. If so, this is evidence that begins to support a claim of discrimination.

Okay. You have your list of facts about people (you, other employees), so let's go to the paper step. What pieces of paper or emails do you have suggesting discrimination? Do you have an email or letter where your supervisor complained about you? Do you have an email or letter where you complained to your supervisor? Where a coworker emailed that she overheard something about you? Do you have a copy of your employee evaluations? Add these bits to your mental or paper list (starting to see the benefit of writing your list down now?). Because paper (or email) does not lie (lawyers say papers "speak for themselves"), this is often the best kind of proof.

With all this information you now have, do me a favor and perform a little experiment. Assume that you are lying to yourself, that discrimination did not take place. What parts of that list make discrimination because of sex more likely to be true? What parts suggest that the employer had a reason for doing what it did that did not involve discrimination? The more parts of your list or memory that suggest discrimination, the more likely it is that you can prove discrimination actually did exist.

So, looking at this list of people and paper, do you think you could prove that discrimination occurred? Do you think your information shows that you did not get the promotion because you are a woman? On the other hand, does it look like your employer had a reason for giving the promotion to someone else that did not involve your sex?

If you think you have proof of discrimination, call an attorney.

How a Lawyer Looks at Discrimination

I wanted to give you a little insight into how a lawyer looks at discrimination. In evaluating a case, the first thing we do is determine what proof of discrimination is out there. We tick off all the things we might need to prove discrimination in our heads and see what is there, what is not there, and how we can attack any reason the employer might have had for doing what it did.

Right now, lawyers apply a variety of legal theories: sometimes we use a motivating factor analysis, sometimes the *McDonnell Douglas* scheme of proof, sometimes mixed-motive analysis, or sometimes another theory. It does not matter what we are doing and you do not need to understand it. We have been warped by years of legal education and practice to think a certain way. Let us have our crazy brains, you do not want them.

You do need to know this. An employer almost always gives a reason for making its employment decision about you. If that reason is true and is not itself discrimination (such as, we fired you because your attendance was poor), then you are unlikely to have a case. So what do lawyers do? We look at the employer's reason and see if it is true. If we can show that the reason is not true, then perhaps discrimination really did happen after all.

Let's stick with that poor attendance example. You will probably know if you were absent from work or not. If you really were absent, does that mean you cannot win? Not necessarily. You need to then look at how the employer treated other employees who were absent. If others were absent around the same number of times and were not fired, then it looks like poor attendance is not really the reason you were fired, right?

Legally, this is called looking for a comparator. We want to know how other people in your same situation were treated. If we can show that you were treated differently or worse than others, then we ask why you were treated differently. If the answer is discrimination (or if the proof suggests discrimination), then you may indeed still have a case.

Other Types of Discrimination

For the most part, we have been looking at how individuals are treated in the workplace and how to prove discrimination resulting from an adverse employment action. There are other types of discrimination cases out there. Two very common ones are harassment and retaliation, and I will discuss those in the next two chapters.

There are also two class action types of cases where groups of people together can make a claim of discrimination. If you feel you are a member of a group of people being discriminated against, please go see a lawyer. Those cases almost always require a sophisticated and detailed statistical analysis to prove a case. As I am not a statistical expert and neither is the typical employee, I will not be discussing these types of cases in any more detail.

Making a Claim of Discrimination

If you think you have a case of discrimination and do not want a lawyer, or cannot get one, then you will probably want to know something about how you can start making a formal claim of discrimination.

First things first. You need to know something about *time limits or statutes of limitations*. Every employment discrimination case (actually, every legal case) has a time limit attached to it, and the time clock starts counting down from the day you are discriminated against. This means that if you wait too long to make a claim of discrimination or file a lawsuit, you may be forever prevented from doing so.

Since that would really, really stink, you want to know your time limits and you want me to tell you what they are, right? Sigh. Every State's anti-discrimination laws can have their own time limits. Federal laws may have different time limits too. Oh yeah, and federal employees can have different ones from private employees. In general, federal employees should contact their agency's Equal Employment Opportunity (EEO) counselor within 45 days of the discriminatory action by your employer.

Non-federal employees, and most cases involving federal law and discrimination claims of race, color, sex, religion, national origin, age, or disabilities, should begin a claim by filing with their local Equal Employment Opportunity Commission (EEOC) office or similar State antidiscrimination office. To do so, you normally just call them up and they send you a questionnaire. You fill it out, sign it, and return it. Usually, the EEOC will review your questionnaire and if they think you have a possible case, they will prepare a formal Charge of Discrimination for you.

This is important. This Charge of Discrimination will need to be filed within either 180 or 300 days from the act of discrimination (fired, not hired, demoted, harassed, etc.). It's 300 days if your State has a nice little State law also prohibiting discrimination, has its own State agency investigating them, and the EEOC considers the State agency as equivalent to the EEOC (the actual term is deferral agency). Most States fall into the 300-day camp. Seriously though, unless you need to, why wait? I recommend filing a charge sooner rather than later.

Once you file your charge, the EEOC will investigate the claim. Sometimes the EEOC thinks you have enough evidence of discrimination, sometimes it does not, and sometimes it can't decide. If you are really lucky, the EEOC will agree to file a lawsuit and represent you. For free.

Let me show you just how biased I am. When this stroke of employment discrimination fortune hits you, I still think you should hire your own lawyer. What? Shark! Bloodsucker! Perhaps. Let me briefly explain. When a lawyer represents you, they only care about getting the best result for you. When the EEOC represents you, they want ... the best result for the EEOC. Sometimes what is best for you and what is best for the EEOC are different. I would say most of the time. Then again, it's hard to pay for something when you get something sort-of like it for free.

Let us suppose that the EEOC has ended its investigation. You know the investigation is over because they sent you a letter in the mail. In this form letter, some boxes will be checked off. One will be if they think you have enough evidence of a claim, another is checked if you don't have enough, and another is checked if they don't know. By far, the EEOC most often makes the decision that they don't know if you have enough evidence to decide yes or no.

What happens now that you have this letter? Keep reading it. It also says that you now have 90 days from the time you receive that letter to file a lawsuit yourself. If you don't, then you have missed your time window and even if you had the best case in the world, there is nothing much you can do about your discrimination claim (you might still have other legal claims besides discrimination, though, so don't cry too much). You can certainly try to represent yourself. By now, you should probably know my opinion: if you think you have a case, I recommend contacting an employment lawyer.

One more thing. When the EEOC ends its investigation, you should immediately write them and ask for a copy of their whole file on your case. You won't get the whole thing because they will remove some information. However, you will still get a lot. In fact, you will get a very good thing. Unbeknownst to you, after you filed the Charge of Discrimination, the EEOC went to your employer and asked for their response. The Evil Employer had to submit a detailed written letter where they explained all the reasons why they did not discriminate against you. This is very useful information, because you want to know those reasons. You want to know them because you just might be able to prove that those reasons are not true or accurate. If you can prove those reasons are false (you remember what I wrote earlier because you hang on to my every word), you go a very long way towards proving employment discrimination.

Okay? Good.

Religion Gets Special Treatment ... Sort Of

Religious discrimination is treated differently than discrimination claims (so are people with disabilities, but that's another chapter). I guess you could say that Congress discriminated in favor of religious people when it passed its laws. All the things I wrote about previously remain true about religious discrimination. At the same time, religious people get a special benefit in our laws. If there is a conflict or problem between an employer's rule and an employee's religious belief, the employer might actually have to change its rule. This is called a religious accommodation.

For example, let's suppose that an employee cannot work on a certain day because of his or her faith, but the employer requires the employee to do so. We have a conflict. Under normal discrimination rules, if the employer requires an employee to work a certain day just like other employees do, he or she has to work on that day. However, in religious cases, the employer just *might* have to let the employee off.

If you think that religious employees are getting some kind of huge gift, you are wrong. The Supreme Court has looked at this and said that an employer only has to make small, minimal accommodations. How small is small enough? Really small. So small that it really does not give that much protection.

Didn't I just write that an employer has to give an employee a religious day off? That sounds like a lot of protection. First, I wrote 'might'. I know these are the kinds of maybes and grey areas lawyers talk about that drive people crazy. Please don't blame us. We are only explaining the law. More specifically, whether or not an employer has to give an employee a day off depends on many things. Does the employer have a seniority system about who works when? If so, an employer normally does not have to change that kind of system, regardless of religious factors. Does an employer have a shift schedule for all employees requiring rotation? Many courts say that employers can require such shift rotations and that no one employee can change that system. However, if an employee does have a flexible staffing system, it just might have to let a religious employee get a benefit from that system.

Please do not misunderstand me. The law does provide some small benefit to religious employees. But not much more than that. At the same time, remember, an employer cannot discriminate against an employee's religion just as it may not do so based on his or her gender, race, national origin, etc. When we talk about disability discrimination and accommodations, you will see that disabled individuals get greater protection, and can get more accommodations, than others.

INTERLUDE

TO THE LEGAL SCHOLARS OUT THERE

I know. I really do. You want to quibble with my words and say there are so many little bits of discrimination law out there that I just skipped over. Yes I did. You want to point out that I did not talk about systemic disparate impact (I briefly mentioned it), affirmative action, mixed motive, multiple decision-makers and the cat's paw, the Equal Pay Act, monetary damages, punitive damages, and limits on the amount of money you can actually recover. You might be frustrated that in other parts of the book I have not mentioned assault and battery, occupational safety and health, vicarious liability, *respondeat superior*, procedural and substantive due process, unconstitutional doctrines, civil rights, minimum wage and overtime, workers' compensation, drug testing, psychological screening, polygraph tests, background checks, alternate theories of defamation, or even alien-probing done at the employer's request. Correct, I am glad you are paying attention. You want to say that one or more courts have disagreed with me about what I wrote. True, but the majority don't. You want to argue that discrimination is very hard to prove and I make it look easy. Perhaps. You want to say that I make it sound like the law is super clear and does not, at times, contradict itself. Sigh. Yes I am.

You see, as I wrote in the Introduction, I am not writing a 12-volume series of books detailing all the intricacies of employment law here. I am painting in broad strokes so that employees know their basic rights, and so they can use this information to help guide them in the workplace. Of course my default advice is, if you think you might need a lawyer, it is better to talk with one. Not all people can do this. So please, work with me. I am sure you would get an A in my course. Minus.

Chapter 5

Harassment and Hostile Work Environment

What is Harassment?

Everyone thinks they know what harassment is. They are wrong. Yes, even you human resource professionals. If someone just called you a really bad name, it's not harassment. If someone just asked you out on a date, it's not harassment. If someone just told a bad joke, it's not harassment. However, each one of these things can eventually become harassment. As a result, many people just take a mental short cut and say that these individual acts are harassment in themselves. Remember, they are not.

You are probably thinking, "Great. What kind of weird way is this to start understanding harassment? By talking about what it isn't?" Sorry. I wanted to help you clear your mind, and make you unlearn what you think you have learned.

Harassment, also sometimes called a hostile work environment, tries to get at discrimination that does not result in one of those *bad things* or adverse employment actions we discussed in Chapter 4, like being fired, being demoted, losing hours, losing pay, etc. Well, some employers may have treated employees terribly but stopped short of making one of those bad things happen. Let's go with an extreme example. This case is actually where the Supreme Court first recognized harassment. Suppose an employee was raped many times by a supervisor. That's bad, right? Really bad. But, did one of the official bad things happen? No. Does this mean that a truly Evil Employer gets away with this? Without harassment law, yes; with it, no.

Of course, you don't have to be raped repeatedly to have a harassment case. Over time, the courts have decided that to have a harassment case, you need to show that, because of some legally protected reason (just like in discrimination law, something like race, sex, religion, disability, age, etc.), someone at work ***severely or pervasively*** did something that offended you to such a degree that it interfered with your job. The Supreme Court further said that a court should consider lots of things, including how frequent the conduct was, how severe it was, whether it was physically threatening or humiliating, and whether it interfered with one's work performance.

In the end, most harassment cases rise and fall on whether the offensive conduct was either frequent and/or bad enough to meet the severe or pervasive requirement. A single act can *never* be frequent, but it might be "severe" or bad enough. For example, a single act of rape might qualify. One bad joke or insult? Let me ask you a question I ask my students: can you think of a single bad joke or insult that would be so bad that the average employee would have trouble doing his or her job because of it? Even if you can, do you think a judge or jury would agree with you? Judges love to think of themselves as particularly thick-skinned (some juries too).

So, one rape can qualify but one insult cannot. Can you see the distinction that courts might be making? Physical acts (punching, kicking, grabbing, touching) are more offensive than just words. Yes, the old schoolyard saying "sticks and stones can break my bones but words will never hurt me" is effectively part of harassment law. I hope our Government did not pay a consultant for that advice.

What this means for you, the employee, is that if your employer or coworkers are just using words to make your life difficult, you will need more of those offensive words than you would if the offensive conduct was physical. Okay, you get that, but how much spoken or physical conduct is necessary? Unfortunately, I can't tell you. No, I am not keeping secrets from you. It is just that there are too many variations from State to State and from court to court for me to give you any specifics. For example, suppose you want to know if being called "stupid" once a week for three months is frequent enough to qualify as harassment. In some States yes, but in others no.

Also remember that it's not just physical touching or insults that can be harassment. Did you just get reassigned and placed next to the bathroom? Did you get the stinky, old metal desk while other employees got nice sustainable-wood ones? Harassment can be any combination of acts and words, whether physical or not. Okay?

I want to point out something now that we will get to in a bit and cover in the very next chapter. Just because one or two or three bad comments or acts do not by themselves equal harassment does not mean that you must remain silent and suffer through it. You might, *might*, want to complain about this behavior. This is very risky though. So keep reading if you are thinking of complaining to anyone.

Is It Always About Sex?

People always ask me whether harassment is just about sexual attraction between a man and a woman. I have to admit, over the years even EEOC investigators have commented that the answer to this question is yes. I want to make it clear, however, that the answer is NO. Harassment law was first recognized in a sex discrimination case, and yes, it was about sexual attraction. But no, harassment is not just about sex or attraction. Harassment law is all about why you are being treated differently. If it is because of some protected reason (such as race, religion, disability, age, whistle-blowing and, yes, sex), then if you can show the other elements of harassment law, then it is illegal.

So, if an employer harasses me because I am Jewish, or Christian, or Muslim, or Hindu, that is illegal? Yes. So, if an employer harasses me because I am a man, that is illegal? Yes. It does not have to be about sexual attraction. If you are being harassed because of your gender, that is enough to make it illegal.

So, if I am a man and my employer harasses me because I am gay, that is harassment too, right? Umm. Well... Okay, no. Current federal law does not say that it is illegal to discriminate against someone because of his or her ***sexual preference or orientation***. This means that if a private employer wants to fire a gay man or woman, that would not violate federal law. It might be against the law of your particular State, however.

Wait just a moment, you might say. If a female employee has sexual relations with a male employee and does not get fired, and a male employee has sexual relations with a male employee and gets fired, how is this not discrimination because of sex? The man and the woman have been treated differently. Logically, this is discrimination because of sex. I agree with you. It is. Unfortunately, most courts disagree with this. The courts have ruled that, when looking at sex discrimination, sexual preferences are simply not protected, and then they stop thinking. At the end of the day, homosexuals are just not protected *because of their sexual preference*. You can use logic all you want, but courts and judges will not see sex discrimination, only sexual orientation discrimination (which is legal according to federal employment law).

Let's get creative (and stereotypical, perhaps even offensively so—I apologize). Suppose a man wears a pink shirt to work. Suppose that man is thereafter called a "fag" or some other insulting term repeatedly over a long period of time. Is this illegal harassment? This is actually tricky, and I think it is likely to get trickier over the next few years as the United States continues to wrestle with same-sex issues.

To address this question, let me ask you another question (you should know this if you read the previous chapter about discrimination). Is it sex discrimination if you fire a woman for acting too much like a man, or not enough like a woman? The Supreme Court looked at this issue and said that sex stereotyping is a form of discrimination because of sex. So, if an Evil Employer acts on a stereotype (some quality or trait that an employer associates with a group) that is linked with a protected category, that can be discrimination. For example, if you refuse to hire an African-American because you think African-Americans are more likely to engage in crime, that is race discrimination. See, that wasn't so hard was it?

Getting back to same-sex issues. If a female employee wears a pink shirt to work, and she does not get harassed but the male employee wearing the pink shirt does, is this harassment because of sex. To me? Absolutely. The man is being treated differently precisely because he is not acting manly enough—that is a stereotype. Do courts think this is illegal discrimination? No. Most courts still simply refuse to accept this kind of argument. So, because courts have already decided that sexual orientation is not protected by federal laws, they put the kibosh on any type of same-sex or sexual orientation issues, even stereotypes. Sorry. Remember, however, that State laws can vary considerably and may very well protect against sexual orientation or same-sex discrimination.

An Employer Has a Powerful Defense

Once we have evidence that you have been harassed, that means the company can be held accountable, right? Unfortunately, this type of thinking is naïve. As I suggested previously, courts tend to love employers, and many courts assume that there are no Evil Employers at all. Our courts have decided that these wonderful job creators cannot always be blamed for the occasional offensive action of their employees. One bad apple does not spoil the bunch, right? Therefore, if a supervisor (not simply a fellow employee) is the one harassing an employee, the Evil Employer has a defense when being blamed for this harassment.

In order to avoid blame for the harassing actions of its miscreant supervisor, an employer must prove that (1) it has an anti-harassment policy that it reasonably distributes and follows, and (2) that the victim employee did not take advantage of that policy or somehow unreasonably failed to avoid the harassment. For those law-loving people, this is known as the *Faragher/Ellerth* defense, named after the two 1998 Supreme Court opinions creating it.

Wow, what a tough defense (that's sarcasm). Evil Employer hires a perfectly lovely employment lawyer to write up a policy, makes employees read it (and sign forms showing that they read it), and then just follows the policy to investigate claims made by the victim.

You got that? Read that last bit again. Does that mean that once harassment takes place, if the employer investigates *after* the employee is harassed and the employer does something reasonable to stop future harassment, that means Evil Employer cannot be held accountable and the employee has to suck up the pain?! Yep.

You see, the reasoning behind this is that it is unfair for an employer to be blamed for the offensive actions of its employees. An employer cannot know everything. It is far better for the employee to carry the burden of being a victim than to make the employer do so. I am being very simplistic here to make a very important point. Just because an employee actually suffers harassment does not mean that the employer can be blamed.

The Supreme Court made this rule up precisely because none of those bad things (firing, demotion, etc.) occurred. It wanted a way to know that the Evil Employer was somehow involved or turned a blind eye to the harassment. The defense gives a court this information. If an employee follows company policy and complains about harassing behavior, and then the company makes that harassment stop, then the system has worked. It is true that the employee has suffered, but it has not suffered one of those bad things. This is all progress. This is not ultimately bad news, right? You wanted the harassment to stop and it did.

Now let's suppose that the harassment did not stop. Has the employer finally shown that it is evil enough yet? Sigh. Maybe. This is certainly one of those times that I strongly advise consulting with a lawyer—it would be very, very helpful. You see, courts do not require that a company or employer be perfect in their response to a claim of harassment. It only has to act reasonably to stop the harassment.

For instance, if you claim your supervisor made offensive comments about you, can the employer fire that supervisor? Yes. Does it have to? No. It just has to make a really good effort to stop the harassment. You are probably wondering what qualifies as a really good effort. Anti-harassment training (you have watched those videos, haven't you?), an apology from the supervisor with a promise that it will not occur again, the supervisor can be transferred, you—yes you—can be transferred, etc.. Any number of things can be a reasonable response to a complaint. I can say a couple of things, though. A response will always be considered reasonable if the harassment stops. That makes perfect sense. Also, whether or not an employer's response is reasonable will almost always depend on the severity and pervasiveness of the harassment in the first place. The more severe or pervasive it is, the more an employer has to do in response.

What about if the supervisor denies the harassment took place, but you say it did occur, and the employer, shockingly, believes the supervisor? Can you hold them liable then? Yes, here you usually can—but remember, you have to provide evidence that harassment actually took place. Do you really have that evidence? Remember, it's not enough just for you to say it occurred.

Guess what? There is a hidden benefit to employees in this defense. Certainly, by pushing employees to complain, the law is trying to get harassment to stop. All joking aside, this is a good thing. However, maybe, just maybe, the supervisor who is harassing you has harassed other people too. If he or she has harassed others, the defense becomes harder for the employer. Unfortunately, I cannot tell you that you automatically win (or lose) here. I can only mention that the defense may not be available depending on how much information about the supervisor is known.

Fine. You are a bit depressed about harassment law. Let's continue with that. Suppose that it is not a supervisor harassing you, but another employee. Does the employer get the defense? Actually no—it gets something better. If the harassment is being done by another employee, to hold the company responsible for that employee's behavior, you have to somehow prove that the company **knew or should**

have known about the harassment and did not take reasonable steps to prevent it. This is very, very difficult. One can sometimes prove this by showing that this co-employee has harassed others, or you or others have warned the company that the harassment is taking place and the company did not react to that information. Like I said, it's difficult.

I need to mention one particular kind of harassment because I do not want anyone to get hurt, legally. If you are physically injured at work due to harassment, you might need to report that harassment or injury immediately. Depending on where you live, harassment law might not even apply to your situation. Why? Because this might now be a type of workplace injury covered by workers' compensation laws, and not employment harassment laws. Any failure to report such an injury might just end up hurting you legally. Best thing to do? Call a lawyer. If you can't find one, consider reporting the injury to your employer as soon as possible. Okay?

Reporting Harassment to the EEOC

I wanted to follow up on my section about Making a Claim of Discrimination in Chapter 4. Remember how I wrote that you have either 180 or 300 days to file a Charge of Discrimination with the Equal Employment Opportunity Commission or other agency? Well, the same thing is true for harassment claims. The thing is, from when do you count? The first act of harassment or the last? Our lovely Supreme Court actually answered this question for us. It said that as long as one act of harassment (you know, those severe or pervasive acts) occurred within the appropriate 180/300-day limit, then the charge was filed correctly. It's always nice to have an easy answer from the courts.

CHAPTER 6

RETALIATION

You are reading this book and absolutely love it. It might just possibly be the best book you have ever read. Take that Shakespeare! Armed with your newfound knowledge, you don your Super Employee cape and proceed to fight your Evil Employer. Kudos to you! You complain to human resources about an offensive joke that the son of the company president just told you. And then suddenly BAM, you get fired. Human resources tells you that one bad joke does not qualify as harassment, and because it's not actually harassment, they can fire you. Evil Employer strikes again. Insert obligatory maniacal laughter.

Is this legal? Umm, well, maybe, but not always. What kind of terrible legal system is this? They claim to give you rights but then don't protect you at all?! Calm down. Let me explain what is going on. It is true that most federal employment laws have an ***anti-retaliation*** part to them. What these parts say is that an employer cannot do something bad to you (one of those bad things like firing, demoting, etc.) or harass you *(1) if you have properly complained, and (2) the employer's retaliation was because of that complaining.* You see, not all complaints are proper, meaning that not all types of complaints are protected. In addition, just like in discrimination cases, you have to prove that the Evil Employer treated you poorly because of your complaining.

You should be familiar with this "because of" language from Chapter 4's discussion of discrimination. I am going to tell you a little secret. Retaliation cases are usually more successful than straight discrimination cases. Why? In my opinion, it's because people want to believe that the world is good, and that discrimination really cannot be all that common. Hmmph. In contrast, everyone understands the desire for revenge. So, even when people do not think discrimination is going on, they can easily believe that an Evil Employer wants to hurt you because you hurt them with your charge of unlawful behavior.

Before talking about the types of complaints that can be protected, I want to say another thing about proving something happened to you because of your complaints. All of the things I said in the discrimination chapter apply here. Please review that section. Back already? Good. I want to add one more thing here. Another piece of evidence suggesting retaliation is the time between your complaint and the company's retaliation. The shorter that time, the more it suggests retaliation. The longer the time, the less it does (if you are in this category, you are going to want more evidence than just being fired six months after you complained).

When Are You Protected?

Okay, let's talk about what you do to get protected by common anti-retaliation laws. I tend to break up proper or protected complaints into two general categories: ***formal*** and ***informal***. ***Formal complaints*** are usually those where an employee actually contacts a Government agency and requests and participates in an investigation into some kind of unlawful activity. Yes, courts are agents of the Government here too. Usually, if you have filed a written complaint with an agency like the EEOC or Department of Labor, or perhaps filed a lawsuit in court, then your complaint is usually protected in this formal category. In fact, this is some pretty super-duper protection. Even if your formal claim is completely false (for example, you perhaps lied to the EEOC), your employer cannot take action against you because of this claim. This seems pretty strong, doesn't it?

Now let's take some of that super-duper protection away. Let's suppose the EEOC is investigating your claim of race discrimination. The employer, obviously annoyed and hating you now, wants to conduct its own kinder and gentler investigation. So, Evil Employer and its henchmen escort you to a nice friendly interrogation room. They don't like what you say here, and they think you are lying. They fire you for lying to them during this private, company-only investigation.

Can they do that? To answer that, let's consider where we are. If you were fired because you had filed a charge with the EEOC, that would be illegal retaliation. Is this what happened? It certainly might be. However, if we accept the employer's story—that you were fired for lying not to the EEOC, but to them—we are now in the world of ***informal complaints***. You don't get super-duper protection. You only get normal protection. You get this protection if you somehow simply engaged in stopping a form of unlawful activity. This can be any type of behavior, but it usually involves making an internal complaint to the company only, or being interviewed by the company, or helping someone else do the same (or helping some other person file a formal complaint).

In answer to my question, the employer cannot do this *if* the reason is really your charge with the EEOC. It comes down to a game of who has more proof. The more proof the company has that their belief that you are lying is reasonable, the more likely it will be that their firing of you will be okay. As a practical matter, however, most companies will not touch you for a while after you have made a formal complaint—you are too radioactive as a potential retaliation lawsuit.

Not all types of employment complaints are protected, though. Which ones are? I wish I could give you clear guidance. I cannot, because the courts are all over the map. The creativity of human beings to break the law is quite impressive too, making this very hard. Add to this that some types of employment laws do not have anti-retaliation provisions in them. Nonetheless, after reading this book or other sources, if you think that a violation of the law has taken place, you have some proof of that, and you have complained, you are likely protected against bad things and harassment. This is an excellent time to speak with a lawyer.

You Can Go Too Far

Here is where we will really talk about the difference between formal complaint protection and informal protection. In the world of formal complaints, you can never really go too far.

Whatever you say and do is likely protected. You can be as much of a jerk as you want, and your employer cannot retaliate against you because you were a jerk during that formal complaint process. My advice here is, please, do not be a jerk if you can help it.

Not so with informal complaints. If you are only helping out informally (including your own internal company complaint), you might lose any protection you otherwise would have had if you behave poorly. The key here is that an employee must always behave reasonably. If you think the company president sexually harassed you, taking a can of spray paint to the office building's exterior to proclaim your victimhood will not be viewed by anyone (courts included) as a reasonable response.

What might be unreasonable behavior? Sometimes it is violating company rules or orders. All of them? Don't hate me, but it depends. It depends on the rule or order, and what you want to do. The company has to be reasonable here too, because if it goes too far, it provides additional evidence of retaliation, doesn't it? As an employee, you also don't want to stop the company from carrying out its business or otherwise interfering with its legitimate needs. Just because you don't like what the company is doing to you does not mean you can stop doing your job or prevent others from doing theirs. The best thing you can do is to perform your job competently. If you feel like you cannot do your job because of how the company is treating you, then you might need to request some time off and even tell the company about this (hopefully, you have talked to a lawyer before this). This is more common than people think. It's okay to be human and hurt. Be reasonable about yourself too.

So What is Retaliation?

We talked about the bad things of firing, demotion, losing pay, losing hours, etc. If the company does this because of your protected complaint, then it has retaliated. If you are being harassed because of your complaint, then it has retaliated. However, more than bad things and harassment are actually prohibited by anti-retaliation laws. In a recent case looking at federal laws against discrimination, the Supreme Court said that if an Evil Employer did something that would make a reasonable employee not want to make a formal or informal complaint, then that is likely retaliation. So, is it retaliation if Evil Employer takes away your company car, or transfers you to another position? Yes.

Let's suppose Evil Employer fired your spouse because *you* complained about harassment. Is that retaliation? Yes. Actually, the Supreme Court says that your spouse now has a retaliation claim against Evil Employer too, even though he or she never actually made any complaint! Who says the Supreme Court hates employees?

For the record, remember that harassment defense that employers got? They get it for retaliation cases too. In this case, if an employer is harassing you but has not done one of those bad things, the employer cannot be blamed if it can prove that (1) it has an anti-retaliation policy that it reasonably distributes and follows, and (2) the victim employee did not take advantage of that policy or somehow unreasonably failed to avoid the retaliation.

You now know how to complain, and when to complain. But what kinds of things can you complain about? According to federal law, here are some common things you can complain about that are related to the workplace: race discrimination, color discrimination, national origin discrimination, sex discrimination, religious discrimination, age discrimination, disability discrimination, workers' compensation, commercial motor vehicle safety, health plans, retirement plans, pension plans, minimum wage issues, overtime issues, reporting Government fraud, requesting or taking medical leave, mine and railroad safety, banking fraud, genetic information discrimination, federal jury service, occupational safety and health issues, and veteran status or military service discrimination. This is not a complete list by any means, and of course States have additional anti-retaliation laws too. Just remember that simply having a law that protects some complaints does not mean that all complaints are protected. Put another way, you can complain about anything you want to your employer, but you can only complain about what you want and get *anti-retaliation protection* (freedom from being punished for your complaining) from only a small subset of things about which you complain.

Careful, Careful—Retaliation and Reporting Harassment

It is worth knowing that reporting harassment can be tricky business. Remember how I said that you get protection by making an informal complaint if you believe that a violation of the law occurred? Well, when does harassment actually occur? Do you have to wait until all the severe or pervasive things have happened before complaining? If you don't wait, and you are wrong, can you be fired?

Let's revisit my first example in this chapter with our newfound understanding of retaliation. Suppose you complain to human resources about an offensive joke the son of the company president just told you, and you get fired. Human resources tells you that one bad joke is not harassment, and since it's not actually harassment, they can fire you.

What do you think? Is this one bad joke enough evidence of actual harassment? Is it close to being severe or pervasive enough? If you are inclined to say yes, think again. The Supreme Court considered one such bad joke, and rather dismissively said that a complaint about one joke did not get protection. Of course, that joke involved sexual innuendo.

Let's consider another actual example. Suppose that a co-employee calls someone on a televised news report a really, really awful name. Let's assume that when another employee complains to human resources about the use of the outrageous and disgusting term, the *complaining* employee gets fired. Retaliation? One federal court said that one use of that word could not reasonably be considered harassment. Thus, complaining about one terrible episode of name-calling was not protected, and the employee could be fired.

Okay, lesson learned. Don't complain until you know for sure that harassment has taken place. Of course, when you complain (meaning you have had to endure harassment), and Evil Employer stops the harassment, the harassment/retaliation defense I mentioned earlier kicks in and Evil Employer walks away safe.

The likely truth is that you do not actually have to wait for a full case of harassment before you complain to get protected. How close do you have to get? Harassment law does not give an easy answer. It says things like "reasonably" close. So, more than one joke or insult. How many more? I cannot say. Sorry.

By the way, you might try to be clever. You might re-read the employer's harassment defense, and notice that the defense is not available if the employee had a good reason for not complaining early. You might try to argue that, because courts themselves have refused to give anti-retaliation protection if you report too soon, that refusing to report harassment early is now a reasonable decision. In other words, can an employee refuse to report harassment and say that their good reason for not reporting it is because of courts refusing to protect them? Good luck with that. While I may just agree with you, courts do not like to be shown that their rulings are inconsistent with justice for employees.

CHAPTER 7

DISABILITIES & ACCOMMODATIONS

Employees who have disabilities get some special protections in employment law. Congress passed the Americans with Disabilities Act (ADA) in 1990 to address longstanding discrimination against disabled people. Unlike other discrimination laws, the ADA ensures that employers must sometimes give disabled employees special treatment. They call that special treatment a *reasonable accommodation*. First things first, however. To get the protections of the ADA, you must have a disability.

Do You Have a Disability?

Technically, you don't need to have a current disability to be protected under the ADA. What you need to do is satisfy one of the three legal definitions of being an individual with a disability to get protected under this federal law. Yes, having an actual, current disability is one of those definitions.

What does it mean to have an actual disability? It is more than simply being diagnosed with some kind of illness, although that is the beginning. That illness must also substantially limit one or more major life activities. Okay. And what does that mean? Well, the Supreme Court tried to answer that question. Congress hated that decision, and overruled the Court by changing the law. Thanks for the legal history lesson, you say? You're welcome. Congress changed the ADA in 2007, so it was not that long ago. I mention this because Congress added a laundry list of things to the ADA in an effort to help define those major life activities that need to be substantially limited by the illness

Do you really want to know what these major life activities are? Alright, here we go. Major life activities are those involving caring for oneself, performing manual tasks, seeing, hearing, eating, sleeping, walking, standing, lifting, bending, speaking, breathing, learning, reading, concentrating, thinking, communicating, and working. But wait, there's more! Major life activities also include the following body functions: functions of the immune system, normal cell growth, digestive, bowel, bladder, neurological, brain, respiratory, circulatory, endocrine, and reproductive functions. In addition, Congress also said that these lists are just the beginning and not actually everything.

Normally, you want to talk with your doctor about how your illness is affecting you. I am not saying that you don't know how your illness affects you. Of course you do. I am saying that your doctor can help you identify the major life activities actually involved, while you can provide actual real-life details as to how those activities are really affected in your life. Your input here is actually critical. Whether or not a person has a disability is determined by looking at each individual person, not just looking at his or her illness or label. By looking at each person on a case-by-case basis, you are trying to see if that person's major life activity is ***substantially limited***.

With apologies to the six-million dollar man, let's suppose you were in a car accident and are, tragically, paralyzed. Now let's suppose that a lovely private philanthropist decided to spend more than six million dollars to give you some robotic implants that turn you into the strongest, fastest person alive. Do you have a disability now? Yes. Did your jaw just drop? How can that be? Hear me out. You see, one of the reasons Congress spanked the Supreme Court on disability law was over eyeglasses. If people have poor eyesight, they have a disability with their sight, correct? But if they put eyeglasses on, that disability is corrected and there is no current "substantial" limitation anymore. The Supreme Court said that when determining whether a person has a disability, you have to look at them as they actually are. If they are taking medications, have surgery, or have other types of treatment that lessen the impact of an impairment or illness, that person no longer has an actual disability. You can see the logic here. If someone has been on medication for five years to treat diabetes, or depression, or high blood pressure, how do we know what he or she will really be like when not taking their medications? Sure, we can guess. We might even have really good guesses. They are guesses, though, and the law hates guesses. So, the Supreme Court said just look at people how they are—no guessing!

This ruling got people really, really mad. Especially people with mental health issues—they were effectively denied the benefits of the ADA by this ruling. Congress responded, and disagreed with the Court. It passed a law saying that you should not consider treatment or anything like it when determining whether someone has a disability. Oh, except for considering eyeglasses—that's still okay.

So where are we? Do we just look at the diagnosis now? No. We still look at how it affects you. We do not consider any helpful medications or medical treatment though. We "guess" at how your major life activities would be affected without such treatment. Practically, this means your doctor will likely be involved in helping you understand any illness and its impact on your life.

This is only one definition of being a person with a disability. There are two more. Another definition is that you have a history of having a disability (but you no longer have that disability now). This is getting at discrimination because of a label. If an employer finds out you once had an illness that was a disability and fires you because of it (or harasses you), that is unlawful.

The last definition is arguably the most important, and the most difficult to prove, in employment law. If an employer thinks you have a disability when in fact you do not, you are considered as having a disability for employment discrimination purposes. This is the "*regarded as*" definition of having a disability. Think about it this way. You actually can do your job, but because of your employer's assumption that you are ill and cannot do your job, you get fired. Without this definition, the employee would have no protection at all (because the employee does not have a disability, right?), and the Evil Employer would just assume people are sick and fire away.

You should now understand that, unlike proving you are a man or woman or African-American or Christian or Iraqi, it is harder to prove you have a disability than other protected categories. Do not simply assume that because you have a diagnosed illness, even one that you think is pretty severe, the law will assume you have a disability. It won't. You will have to work at proving it.

I want to point out that these disability definitions go beyond employment. The ADA addresses many things. If you are inclined to think that one of the above definitions is not fair to an employer, I can sympathize (but not much, they are evil remember). At the same time, the ADA covers things like stores and restaurants too, where people are customers. Do we really want restaurants or book stores to refuse to serve people who once had an illness if they don't have it anymore?

What is an Accommodation?

Once an employee can prove he or she has a disability, all the regular anti-discrimination rules apply. They can't be treated differently because they have a disability (whether this is an actual disability, the person is regarded as having a disability, or has a history of having a disability). Disabled employees also get something else. Remember when we discussed religious accommodations? Well, the disabled may also get accommodations in the workplace.

Here is how the law works. If an employee with a disability can do all his or her essential job duties, then the employee does not get any special treatment or accommodation (the employee does not need any help). If, however, a disabled employee cannot do those duties, but could do them with the help of a ***reasonable accommodation***, then the employer has to make that accommodation. An *accommodation* is nothing more than something that will help the employee do his or her job effectively.

How do you know what accommodations you can get? Start thinking of it this way. What job duties do you have trouble accomplishing because of your disability? Once you have that list, then think of what the employer could do to help you complete those duties. This is another good time to talk with your doctor. Try to think of everything the employer could do. Now look at that list. You might have some super-duper-your-life-will-be-great-now ideas. Guess what? The employer does not have to do them all. It only has to make *reasonable* changes or accommodations (and, the employer is free to come up with its own list of accommodations too). Anything on your list that is very expensive, or changes your job *too much*, or asks too much of an employer, is not considered reasonable. For example, usually, being transferred to another job that might be easier on you is a reasonable accommodation. However, if the company has a seniority system (meaning, it gives job priority to people who have worked for the employer longer than you) that applies to job transfers, that is no longer reasonable. This is another great time to get the assistance of a lawyer. Whether or not something is reasonable can be complicated. If you just can't get a lawyer, then try to get as much help from your doctor. Every little bit helps.

I would like to make sure you understand the difference between accommodations for disabilities versus those for religion. While religious accommodations can only be done if they have a minimal cost or disruption to the workplace, that is not true for disability law right now. Employers have a much greater responsibility to accommodate people with disabilities. If you or the employer can identify a reasonable accommodation that you need, then the employer *has to* give it to you. Has to. The law says it's a kind of discrimination to not give that accommodation.

Of course there are exceptions. The ADA gives employers some extra defenses too. We will only discuss a basic one here. Even if an employee needs an accommodation, the employer does not have to actually provide it if doing so would be too difficult or cost too much money. You can think of it this way—this kind of gives the employer another chance to argue that the accommodation you want or could help you is not reasonable, but the employer actually has to prove it this time. There are nice regulations spelling out things to consider, like the financial resources of a company, the number of employees, etc. For now, let's keep it simple. It's a second chance to show unreasonableness. If it can do that, you don't get the accommodation.

Indeed, most employers will not want to give an employee any accommodation at all. They will try to claim that any accommodation is unreasonable. If you think they are wrong, it is definitely time to contact a lawyer. You just might need to push back, and push back hard.

How Do You Get an Accommodation?

We now understand the basics of the ADA and disability discrimination law. We also know that disabled employees might be able to get an accommodation to help them perform the important or essential parts of their jobs. How do you actually get an accommodation? You have to ask for it. In most places, an employer has no obligation to help you find the accommodation that could help you do your job. If you want help, you have to get it. If you don't ask for it and they fire you for not doing your job well enough, it may just be too late.

This is not always true. The EEOC, the Government agency in charge of employment fairness (or what they think is fairness), claims that if an employee requests a meeting to discuss possible accommodations and the employer refuses, then that is discrimination too. Some courts even agree. Some are very skeptical and don't like the EEOC (or employees) much. At the end of the day, if you need help, ask for it—don't wait for your employer.

It is true that some illnesses actually make it hard for people to ask for help. For example, people with certain mental illnesses may refuse to believe they are sick at all. To force those people to ask for help when their illness convinces them that they need no such help is a recipe for failure. Accordingly, a few courts have said that if an employer has reason to believe that an employee is suffering from such an illness, the employer just might have to begin talks about what accommodations an employee needs. As a lawyer who tries to help mentally ill people, I think this is a very kind idea. Most courts, however, do not agree, and still require an employee to start the process himself or herself.

Federal Employees and Disability Discrimination

I owe a big apology to federal employees. I forced you to read through several boring pages about the ADA. Unfortunately, the ADA does not apply to you if you work for the federal Government. Nice trick, huh? Make everyone obey a law, and then make sure it doesn't apply to one of the largest employers in the nation. Federal employees do get some disability discrimination protection from another law, the Rehabilitation Act of 1973. I think of the Rehabilitation Act as ADA-light. It has similar language, but is just not as specific.

Like the ADA, the Rehabilitation Act gives similar disability discrimination protection to employees like the ADA, just a little less. If you are a federal employee with a disability, you really should contact your EEO counselor or a lawyer as soon as possible. Please.

Sick But Not Disabled

Sometimes, an employee may not have an illness that lasts very long. Short-term illnesses are not disabilities. So, if you get sick and need to miss some work, can an employer fire you? Maybe. It is certainly not right or fair for an employer to do that, but it might be legal unless a federal law applies to them, the ***Family and Medical Leave Act*** (FMLA) or a similar State law.

In order to be protected by the FMLA, a few conditions must be met. First, an employer must have at least 50 employees. Congress made a decision that smaller employers can fire sick people whenever they want. We need to accept that. Second, an employee needs to have worked for the employer for at least one year, and not just part-time (an employee needs to have worked at least 1,250 hours in the past year, actually). If these basic requirements are met, an employee is probably covered by the FMLA. Are there more requirements than these two? Yes. But these two are the most basic, and therefore are the ones that matter to most employees. You can thank me for not going through all the regulations. Really, you don't want that.

So, what does the FMLA get you? In general, you get up to twelve weeks of leave (whether paid or unpaid) to deal with a ***serious health condition*** or issue for you or a close family member. This includes pregnancy. Please note that this protection is for sick leave, not parenting leave. If you have a child who is *not* sick and you need time off work to care for him or her, the FMLA does not protect that time.

You do have to ask for sick leave to deal with a serious health condition, though. What is a serious health condition? This can be a very complicated issue. However, if you or a family member needs a doctor's care or treatment for at least three days, you should be able to meet this definition. Usually, an employer will ask for proof of this illness. This is perfectly acceptable, but only certain information has to be given to them. Hopefully, your doctor can help guide you here. If not, guess what time it is? Time to talk with an attorney.

Also, an employer cannot fire you or punish you for taking this leave. However, many people think that an employer must give you your same job when you return from leave. This is not entirely true. An employer only has to give you a similar position back, and maybe not even at the same location.

These are just the very basics of FMLA law, and there are many, many exceptions. The FMLA is such a complex area of law due to governmental regulations that I really cannot do it justice in this book. I do think it is important, however, for every employee to know at least this little bit about his or her rights. More people get sick than get disabled, after all.

CHAPTER 8

FREEDOM OF SPEECH

I cannot tell you how many employees contact me saying that their Evil Employer has just fired them and it's unfair because they simply told the truth. When I begin to explain employment at-will to them, they are completely shocked.

For whatever reason, as Americans, we tend to grow up thinking that we have the right to say almost anything we want and no one can punish us for that. Actually, I loved that idea. And then I had kids. I realized that there are plenty of good reasons why not every kind of speech should be protected.

Nonetheless, our ideas about being Americans and having free speech are not quite accurate. I hope this chapter helps give employees a more realistic view of their rights to free speech in the workplace.

Private Employees

Okay, private employees, get ready for some bad news. What? You don't know if you work for a private company or not? Well, if you do not work for a federal, State, county, or city Government, or for a public school, public university, public hospital, jail, or Government agency of any kind, then you are probably an employee of a private company.

Back to the bad news. Let me give you a quick summary of free speech rights for employees who work at private companies: ***you have no freedom of speech rights***. Shocking, isn't it? Although that is not quite accurate, it is a very good place to begin. As I wrote, as Americans, we like to think we have free speech rights coming out of our mouths. We don't.

The First Amendment to the Constitution that gives us freedom of speech does not actually say we have complete freedom of speech. It merely says that the *Government* cannot take away our right to freedom of speech (except in some circumstances). It does not say that private employers cannot make us be quiet or say something in the course of our jobs. Evil, right?

Of course, you know that this is not true. We talked about retaliation already in Chapter 6. We know that sometimes employers cannot punish us for what we say if another law protects what we say or do. That is the rub, though. The First Amendment does not really apply to private employees; other laws do.

Aha! You are using your incredible memory (well done) to remember that one change to at-will employment from Chapter 1 was something called wrongful discharge. Is it perhaps possible that the freedom of speech guarantee in the First Amendment is a public policy that prevents you from being fired? It sounds quite promising, doesn't it?

Sigh. For the most part, no, this does not give you any protection. In some States, yes it does. In almost all of them, no. Again, the First Amendment's guarantee to free speech is about Governmental interference, not private actors like people and businesses. Most courts that have considered this question did not think that the federal Constitution and its Amendments gave much protection to private employees.

Consider this example. Suppose Evil Employer tells its employees that they must go out into their communities and tell their neighbors to vote for Candidate X in the next election. Those who refuse are fired. Is this legal under the First Amendment? In almost all States, yes (wait for the big exception coming up). At the same time, remember, you are certainly free to quit that job. Because the First Amendment does not protect against this kind of command from an employer, all States have passed election laws that try to protect against interfering with how people vote in state elections, and the federal Government has passed a federal law protecting how people vote in federal elections, at least in some circumstances. These laws do not simply apply to employers, though; they apply to everyone.

Just remember the basic idea that if the First Amendment does not protect speech, then a private employer can do or say whatever it wants, or it can make an employee say or do whatever it wants, unless a law says otherwise. Outside of political speech (like voting and elections), there is very little speech protection at all for employees of private companies.

One thing to remember is that even if almost all speech is not protected, an employer might still violate anti-discrimination laws. How? Well, if one person is not disciplined for speech but another is, why were those two people treated differently? If it was something protected by discrimination laws, then the discipline might be unlawful. In addition, if an employee says that God wants only Libertarians elected to office, firing an employee for that speech might be religious discrimination. In other words, the employer should always be careful. And you, employee, should be vigilant. Try not to say political things though, okay? Actually, try not to upset your employer at all.

There is another teensy, tiny wrinkle here. There is a federal law preventing employers from interfering with an employee's speech if that speech is related to employment issues or working conditions and directed to fellow workers. The federal law in question here is part of the National Labor Relations Act that protects "***concerted activity***". This law was once about union activity, but it protects speech for non-union members as well. It is just a small bit of protection, but at least it is something. I think of this as the "9 to 5" rule. If you are as old as me and remember that 1980 movie about sexual harassment and revenge, there was a small part where an employee was fired for discussing her salary with another employee. This is the kind of speech that may qualify for protection under this law—the employees were discussing salary issues, and compensation is something ultimately related to labor union issues. Thus, they should not have been fired and may have been able to sue the company. I know it was just a movie, but it underscores how few people really understand employment law. Still, remember that speech in general is not protected. Knowing this, you should be able to protect yourself from putting your foot in your mouth and losing your job.

Public Employees

Have you perhaps guessed the reason why there are exceptions and special rules for defamation or verbal harassment? Want to know a big reason why they are there? It's about the First Amendment. Because we have freedom of speech, the Government cannot simply make laws saying you cannot express yourself and if you do, you can be fined or go to jail. Any speech they would want to stop would have to go "too far" in some way. What is too far? Given the creativity of humankind, we keep inventing new boundaries of speech. And because people have this creativity, the law tries to be flexible in dealing with freedom of speech issues in the workplace.

As we just learned, in general, the First Amendment does not protect private employees, although other State and federal laws might. It does protect people who work for the Government, though. At the same time, public employers have the right to run their workplaces efficiently. The Supreme Court has attempted to explain when public employee speech is protected and when it is not. In evaluating whether a public employee's speech is protected, the first thing to look at is the actual speech—what did the employee say? If the First Amendment protected what the employee said, then we move to the second step.

Okay, but what speech is protected in this first step? To be protected by the First Amendment, an employee's speech must be about a ***public concern***. This means that the employee must be talking about something that concerns the public or people at large, not just the employee himself or herself. For example, an employee who complains about dirty bathrooms in the office is not speaking about a public concern. An employee who complains about corruption in the workplace is addressing a public concern.

Just to be clear (or make things less clear as the case may be), reporting Government corruption is not always a public concern. Sheesh, haven't you read enough of this book to know that the Supreme Court will always squash such naïve thoughts? For example, a prosecutor once complained to his superiors that he thought a criminal defendant's rights might have been violated, but the Supreme Court said that was not protected speech. That's right. A lawyer for the Government thought the Government violated the Constitution, reported this, and this speech was not protected?! Yep. You see, the prosecutor's job was already to report or talk about legal problems with the case, including any violation of a defendant's rights. Thus, this was not an employee speaking about a public issue, this was an employee speaking as part of his job. Big sigh. So, now we know. Even if a public employee complains about something that is important to the public, if an employee's job duties normally include require making complaints, those complaints and that speech are not protected. Does that stink? Think about it. Suppose the Government hires you to investigate corruption. You find corruption and report it. You get fired. Oops. Guess who is not protected by the First Amendment? Nice system we have, isn't it? We are certainly creating proper incentives for good Government, aren't we?

Let's suppose you think you can game this system. Instead of complaining internally, you go straight to the *Washington Post*, or *Wall Street Journal*, or the *Libertarian Blog from Guatemala* and report the exact same thing. Is your speech now protected? Actually, yes. But that only gets us to the next step.

Once you have established that your speech is protected, the Government gets to explain why your speech is so harmful and dangerous—not because of its truth, but because of its interference with normal business operations and efficiency. If you read enough about free speech law, you might hear reference to such things as *Pickering* factors or the *Pickering* test. *Pickering* factors are those things that courts consider when balancing an employee's right to free speech with the Government's needs as an employer. If a court thinks that the Government wins on these factors, guess who loses? You, and any idea of freedom of speech.

So what are the wonderful *Pickering* factors? Before I tell you, please see if you can tell how the more power an employee has to actually make a difference, the more the First Amendment will *not* provide protection. All right. Here are the factors: does the speech (1) hurt the authority of superiors to discipline employees, (2) affect co-worker harmony, (3) damage the close relationship based on loyalty and confidence when necessary to a job, (4) affect the ability of the employee to do his or her job, (5) hurt the regular operation of the Government's business, and (6) come from an employee important to the Government's business (for example, does the person have a confidential, policymaking, or public contact role).

That's quite a list, isn't it? Determining whether the Government or the employee wins this balancing test is done on a case-by-case basis to examine the employee's speech, the actual employee's role in the company, the effects of the speech and so forth. If you have a free speech issue, it's another great time to talk with an attorney.

Can I Be Fired For Being a Republican? Democrat? Libertarian? Independent? Tea Partier? Bull Moose? Socialist? Statist? Member of the People's Front of Judea?

If you work for a private company, the answer to this question is generally yes, as far as the First Amendment is concerned. Political association is related to free speech. Accordingly, the same things I said about private employees and free speech apply here. You don't have much protection in federal law. Hopefully you can find a State law or wrongful discharge claim to protect you. Sorry.

Public employees again get protection. However, if you have a policymaking position (i.e. you are involved in politics and making important decisions about what the Government should do with all our money), you are not protected. The reason the First Amendment does not cover you high-ranking people is because, well, the Supreme Court says so. They said the Government should be able to discriminate politically because the Government is allowed to demand loyalty in those people responsible for pushing a governing party's political agenda. All other public employees are protected. You cannot be fired, demoted, not hired, transferred, and arguably all those other *bad things* we call adverse employment actions because of your political affiliation. Breathe easy, Bull Moosers.

Chapter 9

Employee Privacy

Do you want to know a secret? Your employer does. It wants to know everything about you, from what you have in your social media accounts, what you are typing in your email, what you have stashed in your briefcase, and lots and lots more. Do you have to let them find out? If you are an at-will employee, can they do anything they want? If you refuse, can they fire you?

There are limits to what an employer can do to obtain information about you, and there are more limits on public employers than private ones (surprise, surprise). I will give you a brief overview of this increasingly complex area of employment law.

Employment File

First things first. How can you know what information your employer already has about you? Try to get a copy of or look at your employment file.

Many clients ask me to get their employment files or records for them. People simply assume that a lawyer has a legal wand of some kind that forces employers to cower in fear and instantly cough up all kinds of information. Unfortunately, absent some special laws passed in your State, a private employer has absolutely no obligation to show you anything. And they won't.

Public employees *do* have access to their employment files. That is only because a federal law gives that right to federal employees, and most States have laws giving that right to State and local employees.

Searches—How Criminal Law Applies to Public Employees

Everybody has watched enough television to know that the Fourth Amendment to the Constitution provides that the Government cannot conduct an unreasonable search or unreasonably seize your property without a warrant unless you give them permission. You might be surprised to know that the same general rules apply to Government employees as well. That's right, you have the same rights as criminals. Actually, public employees have fewer rights.

Guess what, though? Remember how we talked about free speech and those *Pickering* factors? Well, a similar analysis applies to Government searches. Instead of wondering if your speech was about a matter of public concern, in privacy issues, we start by wondering if you had a ***reasonable expectation of privacy*** in the thing to be searched. This means that if our current, modern society would conclude that the thing to be searched is private, you have a reasonable expectation that it is private, and you can go to the next step in deciding whether it really is private. By the way, determining whether you have a reasonable expectation of privacy is the exact same beginning step for criminals as well. This is our Fourth Amendment in action.

What sorts of things does our society think is private? As usual, the actual law is not that helpful. You may have guessed by now, and have probably seen, that the law rarely gives an absolute yes or no answer to anything. The law needs some flexibility to deal with the unknown future, and that flexibility leads to things being vague at times. It's a price we pay for living under the rule of law while having human beings and not angels run things.

Okay, we are not angels. Got it. So how about something to help us know if we have some privacy already? As I suggested above, when it comes to privacy claims, the law likes to look at each specific case individually. In doing so, however, some common themes have emerged from courts as they wrestle with these questions. One way to know if you have a privacy right in something is whether or not other people have access to it. For example, did you leave your briefcase by the front door? Another thing to consider is where you actually kept your property. Did you keep it in an area that has a private use, like a locker? Did you take any steps to seek privacy in any way? For example, did you put your own lock on something? For electronic information, do you have your own password to keep information away from others? Is that password yours or did the Government tell you to create it? You can see that what the law looks at is how a space or your property is actually being used, not how it might be used. So, if you want something to be private, take steps to make it private.

Another thing to consider is whether the Government has a workplace policy about privacy that gives you some private or personal space. If they do, how clear is that policy? After reading the small list of things to think about above, you can see how difficult it is to actually say, X is private or Y is not private. Why? Because all workplaces are different. We need to be flexible, and flexibility means fewer answers that are correct all the time.

Even with a reasonable expectation of privacy, the Government can still violate that privacy. It can do so if it has a search warrant or just a really good reason. What's a good reason? As with freedom of speech issues, one good reason is the Government's need to run its operations in an efficient way (try to avoid jokes here), or the need for the reasonable supervision and control of employees. The key here again is whether the Government is acting reasonably. Great! Another test for reasonableness. Who knew that being reasonable could create such headaches?

How do we know if the Government is acting reasonably? First, do they have a warrant? If they do, sorry, it's reasonable at least until a judge says it's not. Second, is the Government searching for information related to a crime or just workplace misbehavior? If the Government is investigating a crime, they need a warrant. If they are investigating workplace violations, they do not. Finally, not every kind of search related to a workplace violation is constitutionally acceptable. For this type of search, the Government must have information suggesting that evidence of workplace misbehavior or work-related property is located in the place to be searched, but they must have this information before they begin the search. The Government must also only search those areas likely to have the items they think are there, and can only conduct their search in a reasonable way that is not overly intrusive.

The key point to remember is that, without a warrant, a Government employer can only conduct a reasonable search related to workplace misconduct or to retrieve Government property. Anything else is likely to be a violation of your Fourth Amendment rights.

Invasion of Privacy

The private Evil Employer laughs at the Government's inability to search its employees. It wants to find out as much about you as possible. Without a Fourth Amendment that applies to them, what is to keep them from searching your purse, your locker, your desk, your filing cabinet, your clothes, your body, or your life? In other words, what keeps your Evil Employer from invading your privacy? Well, I am glad you asked.

If your employer is nosy about what you are doing at work, they might go too far and commit the tort of *intrusion upon seclusion*. It even rhymes. This tort is somewhat similar to the Fourth Amendment as explained above. In this case, if you have a reasonable expectation of privacy in something, if you have not agreed to let the employer conduct the search, and if the actual search would be highly offensive to a reasonable person, your employer may have invaded your privacy and you can hold them accountable.

Is this common? No. First of all, many States have not accepted that this tort even exists. Second, those employers who are likely to want this type of information simply inform employees that they have no privacy, and their belongings can be searched.

Suppose you log into your private email account —not the one your employer gives you—while at work. You read email about your life. One of those emails is from a recruiter who happened to find you on a social media site, and has a job offer that doubles your salary if you are willing to move to Nigeria. You trash that spam and hope no one falls for it. Guess who does fall for it? Evil Employer hauls you into its cold interrogation room and asks if you are planning to leave the company and go to Nigeria. You deny it. They show you a printout of the Nigerian email. They call you a disloyal liar and fire you. You are an at-will employee, so they can do this right? But they just stole your private email!

Good question, isn't it? And all too common. Let's do what lawyers do and analyze this. Do you have a reasonable expectation of privacy here? You will probably say something like, "Hey stupid, it's MY email, that sure is private isn't it!" Trouble is, did you use the company's computer to access that email? Did you use the company's server and internet connection to access that email? Isn't it possible that viruses can be in emails (or attachments, or links to viruses, or whatever the next great virus uses) and that you can harm the company's property by using your private email? The courts that look at scenarios like this usually agree that there is no way you can have a *reasonable* expectation of privacy in your electronic information when you are using your employer's property. Oh, and I see your brain thinking. What if I use my own private smartphone, huh? Well, are you still using your employer's wireless network and server? I will agree that if you have a private smartphone, and use your telephone provider's data service, then this is more likely to be private. Otherwise, most courts will probably think there is no privacy claim for you here.

With relatively new technology (yes, in the law, the internet is considered new technology), it can be tricky trying to guess what is reasonable. What might have been private yesterday is not private today, and vice versa. This is how the law develops, by analyzing these questions case by case, and refining what is and is not private over the years. Why do things that were once private cease being private? Because the idea of what is a *reasonable* expectation of privacy is an objective one, a societal opinion, and that can change over time, sometimes even quickly (think about how everyone with their own smartphone likely now can be tracked by satellite (GPS)).

Oh, one more thing should be said. Now that you have read about this, do you think it's ever a good idea to email a lawyer about how your employer is evil while at the time using the company's own property (network, computer, or smartphone) to send it? No, it is not a good idea. Yes, I get emails like this all the time, often from the email account provided by the company. I wish people would not do that.

You Just Searched What? More on IIED

Do you like how I snuck one of those lawyer acronyms in on you? IIED stands for the tort of ***intentional infliction of emotional distress***. Remember when we discussed that in our first chapter? Sometimes an employer can behave so poorly, so outrageously, and so shockingly badly, that they must be punished. This sometimes comes up in privacy settings as well.

In its attempt to get information, an employer may just engage in terrible, shocking behavior that results in actual emotional or physical harm to you. Remember the strip-search? Despite what I write in this chapter about employee privacy, just remember that if an employer is behaving not just badly, but incredibly terribly, they have likely committed this tort and can be held accountable. Unlike intrusion upon seclusion, most States recognize the IIED tort. As I wrote in Chapter 1, however, it is rare that courts think that something was truly terrible. They are quite permissive of other people's pain, you know. It is still worth remembering.

Love, Employment Style—Employee Relationships

When we were talking about invasion of privacy matters and the intrusion upon seclusion tort, we never really talked about whether the employer could interfere with an employee's private conduct outside of work. In those States that recognize the intrusion upon seclusion tort, you usually have a reasonable expectation of privacy in your private life and home. If you do not give the employer consent and they invade that privacy (by recording it, by searching it, or by just being there), and if that invasion is highly offensive, the employer is likely to have committed the tort, and you can hold them accountable.

This rarely happens, though. You know what is more common? An employer simply tells you what you can or cannot do in your private, spare time.

Let's say the employer wants you to stop volunteering to help AIDS victims or any other group, or it wants you to stop dating the love of your life who happens to work for a competitor. If you refuse, the employer fires you. Is this an invasion of privacy? What have they invaded? You are an at-will employee, after all. You can certainly leave the job instead of giving up another important part of your life. The private employer is free to run its business how it sees fit.

Actually, the example where an employee was fired for helping AIDS victims was a real court case. The employee lost, meaning the employer was allowed to fire her because she refused to stop helping victims during her non-working time. Courts seem reluctant to create privacy rights that interfere too much with the at-will employment relationship.

However, what about our love story example? Can an employer interfere with romantic choices? Actually, most courts suggest the answer is … yes. Employers can fire people for simply dating another person? Yes. All the time, in every State? No. Whew. Those States that prevent an employer from interfering in private choices have usually passed a law or statute preventing employers from doing this. States like California, Colorado, New York, and North Dakota have passed lifestyle laws preventing employers from interfering with an employee's lawful off-worksite activities. Other States have found that employer interference in private relationships sometimes can be so outrageous that the particular interference satisfies the intentional infliction of emotional distress tort.

In short, it's hard to know when an employer will cross the line between permissible interference with your private life and impermissible interference. In other words, when an employer attempts to interfere with a relationship or private conduct, please seek out a lawyer. It is a very complex situation.

Privacy in Electronic Information

In this section, we will talk about what privacy rights people may have regarding their electronic information, such as in emails, computers, cloud storage, social media sites, etc. Back in the day, the Government and employers would use fancy technology like telephone surveillance and wiretaps to collect information on people. They still do it today, even if the technology is so 1950s.

In the 1960s, Congress responded to at least a decade of monitoring abuse by passing a law called the Wiretap Act. After time and technology marched on, Congress passed the Electronic Communications Privacy Act (ECPA) (pronounced "eck-puh") in 1986. The first section of ECPA deals with how people can and cannot intercept or disclose electronic communications. The second section of ECPA is called the Stored Communication Act (SCA). The first part of ECPA deals with information that is currently being transmitted, and the second part (SCA) deals with the information after it has already been sent and is now stored somewhere (like on a server or computer).

Law schools have entire courses devoted to just this area of the law. What does that tell you? No, it's not about driving up tuition costs. Yes, it's because it can be very complicated. In short, anytime

Congress gets involved in trying to fix things, life gets complicated and, surprise, lawyers are needed.

ECPA provides that it is illegal for anyone intentionally to intercept or try to intercept any wire (think telephone), oral, or electronic communication. Okay, now we're talking. You can't read my email, oppressive Evil Employer! Oh, but let's give businesses a huge, honking exception, thought Congress. It's not illegal for an employer to monitor computer use if it normally does so for work performance purposes or if it is simply monitoring the computer service that it provides to employees. Okay. So it's not illegal under this law for an employer to spy on employees who use company computers or for work performance purposes. Yep. Super-protective law for employees? No.

Let's just suppose the law does somehow protect your information. Can an employer ask an employee to sign a form consenting or agreeing to let the employer monitor the employee's wire, oral, and electronic information? Yes. Yes it can. Do employers actually do this? Yes. Yes they do. It's often in the employment manual too. Sigh.

Interestingly, States have not been content to let Congress have all the fun here. Some States have passed laws about electronic information and computer use, and sometimes these are even criminal laws. This makes things difficult for employers who operate in more than one State. Something that might be legal under federal law, and legal in Pennsylvania, might be illegal in Virginia. In short though, assume you have no privacy and act accordingly. You will be better off for it.

Passwords and Social Media

In the last section, I talked about States jumping in to have fun with electronic information. As I write this, States are now jumping in to pass or are considering passing laws preventing Evil Employers from asking employees to consent to searches of their social media sites, like Twitter, Facebook, etc. The concern is that employers might require employees to turn over their login information and passwords for such accounts as a condition for being hired or for continued employment in their current job.

Yikes! You just blasted your supervisor for the jerk's incompetence in a recent post. While the post definitely is high art, especially considering your creative use of alliterative swear words, you just might get fired if that is read. What to do? Freedom of speech? Intrusion upon seclusion? Unlikely. Super States to the rescue. Maryland has already passed a law preventing things like this, and other States are considering it, as is Congress.

There is a lesson here, for all my readers. If employers were already prevented from doing this, or if it was so outrageous or unreasonable, would we need new laws to be passed? I think we can assume that, at least in those States considering passage of these new laws, those lawmakers believe that it is currently legal for employers to do this even if they believe it is extremely unfair. This should make everyone consider how they use such social media sites.

Again, you may think that an employer asking for such information is unfair. I agree. You may think it should be made illegal. Fine. Employers can be creative. Suppose, as a condition of employment, you agree to (1) "friend" a member of the human resources department on your accounts, (2) agree to never mention the employer in a negative way, and (3) you agree to inform the employer whenever you mention the employer in any post, whether positive, neutral, or negative. I ask you: should the law make any or all of this illegal? And if you lie and the employer finds out, can they fire you for lying? Oh, and if these laws prohibit asking about private information beyond simply logins or passwords, what does *private* mean? If you share information with 500 people on Facebook, is that really private?

My point is that when it comes to technology, privacy issues pop up all the time, and changes are happening. The law may not respond quickly enough, or even accurately, to these technological changes. The Supreme Court is even a little wary of deciding too many things based on technology (yes, I think they are a little bit scared or nervous about how technology is changing society and what it means for the law). It is very likely that by the time this book is published, we will already have a host of new laws to consider, or perhaps none. No matter what, I encourage all employees to exercise discretion. All the time. It may be unfair, but it's smart.

CHAPTER 10

QUICK & DIRTY UNEMPLOYMENT LAW

A really bad thing happened. You were fired. You have no savings and no other job lined up. Welcome to our times. Just because you were fired and the employer really, really hates you and thinks you are the worst employee ever does not mean that you just lost everything. You probably just lost about one-third of your income. Let me explain about unemployment benefits.

Our unemployment system was created in 1935 as part of the New Deal. Why do we have unemployment benefits? It's hard to put it better than the Supreme Court did in 1951: "to provide temporary financial assistance to [workers] who became unemployed without fault on their part." This short-term payment to employees is meant to help them stay afloat while they look for new jobs. As we are also finding out, it is also meant to stabilize our national economy during a recession. It is not a policy meant to fight poverty.

I am not going to quote tax structures to you, explain how much an employer has to pay, or tell you about how unemployment is a joint federal-State program. I will say that each State runs its own unemployment program. So, while each State has to follow national minimum standards, each State is still free to do what it wants above those minimums. This means, again, that each State's unemployment system will be different from another State's. It also makes it difficult for me to explain how unemployment will work in *your* State. Therefore, I must write in generalities, and try to help you understand some basic points about what most employees care about—getting benefits.

In order to receive unemployment, employees have to satisfy certain requirements of a State's law. In general, in determining whether an employee can get unemployment benefits, a State will look at how long an employee worked for a company, how the employee stopped working, and if he or she is looking for a job. Accordingly, if you are a new worker, are a part-time worker, quit your job, or are not looking for work, you may not be able to get unemployment benefits. Most fights over whether an employee can get benefits are, therefore, about (1) whether an employee is looking for a job, (2) whether the employee voluntarily quit, or (3) whether the employee misbehaved.

Looking for Work

Let's look at the first of these three. Why do our laws have a requirement that an employee look for a job? The law wants to put pressure on employees to go out and find a job now, rather than only begin to really search after their unemployment payments run out. So, in order to get benefits, you need to look for a job. And you have to really look, not just fake it.

Yes, I have seen the *Seinfeld* episode where George Costanza tried to manipulate the unemployment system. It was funny. It is not funny when people tell the truth and still get denied unemployment. Think on this real example. A man worked for a company for 15 years. He got laid off but thought his old company might hire him back in the future. This man applied for unemployment and got it. He then went on a job interview. The prospective employer said that it would consider hiring him, but they wanted to know whether he would leave them for his old company if they came back to rehire him. The man said yes because he would have years of seniority there. The prospective employer did not hire him, and his unemployment benefits were denied. Why? For telling the truth. The State unemployment agency decided that his truthful answer showed that he was not serious about wanting a new job. Unfair? You bet. Should the employee have lied? Of course not. It goes to show you that simply wanting a new job and searching for it does not always guarantee that you will receive benefits.

What should you do? Take the new job. Who knows what will happen in the future. I am sure if you win the lottery you would quit the job too. Don't get pulled into someone else's vision of the future. Make your decision only now, not about the future that may not happen. In the here and now, you want a job. Right?

Quit or Be Fired

One of the other major reasons that employees do not get unemployment benefits is if they quit their jobs and do not have a good reason for doing so.

Let's look at what happens to a huge number of employees. Evil Employer decides to fire you. They tell you sweetly that they don't want you to have to admit to another company that you were fired, so why don't you just quit or resign instead. You take that sweet option. Uh oh. Have you just voluntarily quit and lost unemployment benefits? Generally, no. Almost all States have decided that quitting in the face of being fired is (1) not *voluntarily* quitting or (2) not quitting at all. You can rest easy here.

What are some good reasons for quitting? Let me start by saying that there are not that many, and they are usually decided on a case-by-case basis. Can you quit to care for a sick child and still get benefits? This is not so clear. The States do not agree that this is a good reason for quitting. What about pregnancy? Can you quit if you get pregnant? Same thing. You see, the States do not agree about whether family reasons or choices are good cause, some yes and others no. I cannot give you a clear answer. Therefore, before quitting your job for a family-related reason, you should find out if your State will give you unemployment benefits. At the same time, don't forget the Family and Medical Leave Act (FMLA) we discussed in Chapter 7 (the *Sick But Not Disabled* section) if you have to leave work temporarily to care for yourself or a family member.

What if your spouse needs to move for his or her job? Can you quit yours and get unemployment? Why do you keep asking me such difficult questions? The answer is, again, it depends on the State in which you live. Some States say yes, some say no.

Fine! Can you tell me anything that is not "it depends"? Actually, no. Remember, I said that each State can make its own decisions about who is or is not eligible for benefits. I will say this. In general, good cause usually includes quitting because of harassment, domestic violence threats, forced retirement, going to school, illness, military service, and a new job that was to supposed to start but surprisingly did not (such as if a new employer offered you a job so you quit your current job, but then the new company took back its offer). Again, before you quit for any reason, if at all possible, either talk to a lawyer or find more about the regulations surrounding unemployment in your State.

Bad Employee—Misconduct

Sometimes, your employer will not give you the choice to quit or be fired, and they just flat out fire you. Even if this happens, you might not be able to get unemployment if you have done something seriously wrong. In unemployment cases, this serious wrong is called ***willful misconduct***. Simply making mistakes at work is not bad enough—we are all human and thus make mistakes. If you cannot do your job well, you can get fired, but it is not a reason to deny benefits. After all, an employee who loses his or her job is precisely why we have unemployment benefits.

Willful misconduct is usually something like breaking a company rule, refusing to listen to your supervisor (insubordination), not showing up to work (absenteeism), or drug and alcohol use. These are the big four most common reasons. When it comes to absenteeism, however, there can be some wiggle room. If you have to miss work because you need to care for a child or family member, courts have sometimes ruled that that kind of absenteeism is not misconduct, and you might get benefits.

In most cases, though, employees tend to know if they have messed up enough at work that the reason they got fired is not just failing to do well but actual misconduct. I hope that knowing this will help employees correct any misconduct before they lose their jobs and their entitlement to unemployment.

Chapter 11

When Should You Hire a Lawyer?

When should you contact a lawyer? If you can, every single time you have a legal question. Really? Yes. Why? Because if you try to understand the law on your own, odds are, you will make a mistake that can seriously hurt you. Seriously. How serious? Serious as in while you may actually have had the best case in the world and could have recovered millions of dollars from Evil Employer, now you get nothing and have no case.

But, you say, you just educated me on basic employment law, can't I represent myself? The answer is no. I have not tried to make you an employment lawyer. I am simply trying to inform you of your general rights as an employee in the hopes that it will help you as an employee. This book is not meant to guide you through an employment lawsuit. The assistance of an experienced lawyer is, in my completely biased opinion, invaluable. Not only does he or she know the law and its intricacies, he or she can also be creative when analyzing the strengths and weaknesses of your case. A lawyer knows more than just employment law, he or she knows the law of evidence and how to put on a trial. He or she knows how to increase legal protection for you during a lawsuit, and how and when to make other tactical and strategic decisions.

I have been teaching law students for almost ten years now. They are bright, industrious students. They want to learn. They are focused. If nothing else, they want to get a good grade. They spend months pouring over detailed materials. When it comes time to apply the employment rules they have studied to relatively simple situations during an exam, it gets really, really difficult for them to apply things correctly—they make mistakes. My point here is just to remind you that employment law is complex. What may seem simple when it is explained is actually quite complicated in reality.

It is worth noting that employment law is not like personal injury law. In a personal injury case, you know someone has been harmed and you know who caused it. Most of those cases are just about how much money an injured person gets to recover, not about whether that person can even recover a single dollar. As you know by now, the situation is very different in employment law.

With all this in mind, I will suggest some times when it is a *really* good idea to do whatever you can to contact a lawyer. You should talk with a lawyer:

- Whenever you think you need to (that one's really helpful, isn't it? It's the best advice here, though.)
- When you do not understand what is happening to you at work and your employer is not communicating well with you.
- When you have lost your job and think it was against the law.

- When you have suffered a *bad thing* at work and think it was for an unlawful, discriminatory, or retaliatory reason.
- When you have complained about harassment and it has not stopped.
- When your employer is investigating you for anything.
- When your employer is lying about you.
- When your employer is treating you in an offensive and outrageous way.
- When you have an employment contract to review.
- When your employer has asked you to sign a settlement agreement.
- When your employer wants you to sign any paper where you release it from a lawsuit or legal claim.
- When your employer asks you to sign a non-competition agreement.
- When you want to see if you can get out of a non-competition agreement.
- When you need a disability accommodation that you do not think your employer will give you.
- When your employer is invading your privacy.
- When you get hurt on the job.
- When you need to take medical leave but your employer denies it.

Top 10 Tips to Employees

We are nearing the end of this book, my lovely readers. When I give talks to other lawyers, I always try to end with a little list of pointers. I will show you the same courtesy. Here are my top 10 tips for all employees to remember:

(1) Obey first, grieve later. This is one of the basic rules of labor and employment law. I don't want you to get fired for insubordination while you try to decide whether your employer just asked you to do something for an unlawful reason. When in doubt about what to do, listen to your employer and do what he or she says. You can complain about it later while you still have a job.

(2) Know your deadlines. Almost everything in the law has a time limit. A potential lawsuit has a time limit by which it has to be filed. A charge of discrimination has to be filed within a certain number of days. A grievance has to be filed with your employer to protect yourself. If you do not know these and other time limits, how will you know if you have already waited too long? So, please try to find out your time limits and act as soon as possible.

The internet is not a perfect replacement for speaking with an attorney about deadlines. With the information in this book, however, you should probably be able to create a nice simple internet search that might find your time limit. Here is a sample search to get you started: "statute limitations Pennsylvania defamation". Feel free to change the terms as you see fit.

(3) Ask to review your employment file. As you know from earlier in the book, public employers usually have to give you access to your employment file if you request it. Private employees, well, you

get what they give you. I also think that you should not just wait for bad things to happen before asking to see your file. Make it a regular thing, sort of like a maintenance check. You take your car in for an oil change routinely, so why shouldn't you ask to check your file routinely? I dare say that your job is more important than your car.

(4) Request your file from the EEOC. If you filed a charge of discrimination with the Equal Employment Opportunity Commission (EEOC) or your State agency and they dismissed your claim, write them a letter and ask for your file. You will get valuable information, including a detailed explanation of the Evil Employer's side of the story.

(5) Human Resources is not your friend. I am not trying to be mean to all the wonderful people who work in human resources or personnel departments. But at the end of the day, this department is there to protect the company and make sure it runs smoothly, not protect you. Do not make the assumption that they will.

(6) Fired? Ask your employer to agree to unemployment benefits. People do not like confrontations. This is why people think lawyers are not people, because we look forward to them. When your employer is firing you, there just may be a little bit of guilt. If you ask them to not fight your eligibility for unemployment, they may agree. While that may not be a legally binding agreement, it might give you peace of mind knowing that some money will be flowing into your household in the short term.

There is another reason to do what you can to get unemployment benefits. If you were fired or had to leave your former employer for, let us say, less than glowing reasons, what will you say in your next job interview? If you are receiving unemployment, this is a small signal to a future employer that, at the very least, you were not fired for willful misconduct. Sometimes, that little bit of information can be the difference between getting the job and not.

(7) Write down things that happen to you at work. This is not about being paranoid, this is about protecting yourself. As I wrote in the discrimination chapter, there is a risk that if you write down what happens to you at work that, if you ever end up in court against your employer, the Evil Employer can get these notes from you. Fine. That is a small price to pay for having good notes about what happened so you do not have to rely on your memory later. Trust me, there is a very good reason that your employer takes notes after meetings with you, and it is not about being nice and remembering that great joke you told either.

(8) Read the employment manual. Even employment defense lawyers will agree with me that this is a good idea for employees. You need to know what your employer says it will do, and what it thinks it can do. This is the best place to start.

(9) It is not your job to improve the lives of your co-workers. This might sound dark, jaded, and skeptical. Yes. Lawyers are professional skeptics if nothing else. I often get calls from people who have

just been fired because they were the problem employee. They complained about things that would help improve the general workplace. They complained about how other people were not efficient. They complained that other employees were not following the "rules". These types of people lose their jobs more than others. Why? Because of at-will employment. Without any job security, whenever an employee complains about something that is not protected by law (retaliation, whistle-blowing, freedom of speech), that employee can be fired. Eventually, that employee will be. Do you want to be that person? If you do, or if you don't care if you lose your job, go get 'em! I like people like you. Make the world a better place. Just remember that life is not fair and don't expect the law to protect your job.

(10) When in doubt, please call a lawyer. Okay, who did not see this tip coming? If you have questions after reading this book about your job in real life, contact one of us. We are not all bad. Some of us actually like people!

Chapter 12

ONLINE RESOURCES

When I was in law school, we took classes in how to do legal research just by using books. Really! It was an honest-to-goodness skill to find information in a library with bits of information scattered in hundreds of different books. I swear dinosaurs were still hiding out in those dark corners.

Time marches on, and all things change. Now, attorneys do research on the internet just like you. While we often use specialized online databases for lawyers, there is plenty of free information out there as well. Here are some legal resources that I believe may help you understand more about your rights as an employee. Have fun!

Feel free to check out these resources on your own, or search for the laws and regulations on the internet. Please keep in mind that the links below were accurate when this book was published. Over time, material on the internet often gets reshuffled and links may no longer work.

General Resources

You want to read a particular *law* or statute passed by ***Congress***? Really? Okay. Here are some websites to help put you to sleep (or give you a headache).

Cornell's Legal Information Institute
http://www.law.cornell.edu/uscode/text

US Code from the Federal Government
http://www.gpo.gov/fdsys/search/home.action

Want to read even more about *federal* laws? Well, how about reading the literature that is agency *regulations* where they try to flesh out and explain those statutes you just read.

US Code of Federal Regulations
http://www.gpo.gov/fdsys/browse/collectionCfr.action?collectionCode=CFR

Did you learn about a particular *court case* that you want to read? Here are my favorite free places to find and search for them.

Google Scholar
http://scholar.google.com/
(make sure you click the legal documents button)

FindLaw
http://www.findlaw.com/casecode/

Here are some good places to help you find information about **State laws and courts**.

FindLaw
http://www.findlaw.com/casecode/

HG Legal Resources
http://www.hg.org/usStates.html

The ***Equal Employment Opportunity Commission*** has plenty of material on discrimination laws and retaliation. In addition to their basic information, I highly recommend exploring the field manuals they have for their investigators. They have very good explanations of the law here.

Basic Laws and Guidance
http://www.eeoc.gov/policy/ada.html

The ***Department of Labor*** also has some very helpful material. You may want to check out these websites.

Basic DOL website
http://www.dol.gov/

Occupational Safety and Health Administration
http://www.osha.gov/

Unemployment Insurance
http://www.dol.gov/dol/topic/unemployment-insurance/

Minimum Wage Issues
http://www.dol.gov/whd/minimumwage.htm

Health Plans
http://www.dol.gov/dol/topic/health-plans/cobra.htm

ERISA and Pension Plans
http://www.dol.gov/dol/topic/health-plans/erisa.htm

Remember in Chapter 8 when we talked about freedom of speech and *concerted activity*? Well the National Labor Relations Board has created a website just to explore this topic.

> https://www.nlrb.gov/rights-we-protect/employee-rights or
> http://www.nlrb.gov/concerted-activity.

Sometimes clients ask me why I am doing something. Usually, it is because a court is making me follow its rules. If you want to know the rules that federal courts have, you can find them here:

> http://www.uscourts.gov/RulesAndPolicies/FederalRulemaking/RulesAndForms.aspx.

Finally, if you want to geek out on the law like I do, feel free to listen to actual Supreme Court arguments here:

> http://www.oyez.org/issues.

ABOUT THE AUTHOR

Wow. I am impressed. You actually read all the way to here and still want to know more about me. Somewhere, I just won a bet.

I represent employees in their work-related troubles. I have been practicing employment law for a long time, and teaching it to law students in Virginia since 2003. I live and work in Virginia, one of the most employer-friendly states in the country, but otherwise quite a lovely place.

Index

Accommodations
    disability 67, 93, 95-100
    religion 66-67

Adverse Employment Action 53-56
At-Will Employment 7-12
    contracts 13-17
    employment manual 16-17
    torts 17-22

Circumstantial Evidence 55-56, 58
Class Action Discrimination 49, 62
Common Law 21, 22
Complaints (*see* Retaliation or Whistleblower)
Concerted Activity 108, 144
Contract 8, 9, 14-17
    at-will employment 8, 9, 14-17
    non-competition agreement 41-47
    term employment 8-9

Defamation 27-39
    intent 35-36
    opinion 31-33
    truth 31
Direct Evidence 54-55
Disability Discrimination 93-103
    accommodations 97-100
    definition of having a disability 93-97
    interactive process 100-101
    major life activity 93, 94

Different Treatment (see Discrimination)
Discrimination 49-67
    adverse employment action 53-56
    age 51
    bad thing 53-56
    charge 63-66
    class action 49
    color 51
    disability 51, 93-103
    evidence 56-60
    filing 63-66
    gender 51
    harassment 71-81
    national origin 51
    pregnancy 51 (*see also* sex discrimination)
    proof 56-61
    race 51
    same sex 74-76
    sex 51, 74-76

Employers
    They are not really evil. Not all of them.
Employment Manual 16, 138
Employment File 113-114
Evidence
    circumstantial 55-56, 58
    direct 54-55
    discrimination 56-61
    employment file 113-114

Freedom of Speech 105-112
    private employees 105-108
    public employees 109-112

Gender Discrimination (*see* Sex Discrimination)

Harassment 71-81
    Complaint 76-81
    employer's defense 76-80
Hostile Work Environment (*see* Harassment)

Intentional Infliction of Emotional Distress 18-20, 119-122
Intentional Interference with a Business Expectancy 36-39

Libel (*see* Defamation)

Medical Leave 101-103
    see also disability

Privacy 113-125
    electronic information 122-123
    searches 114-117
    social media 124-125
    torts 117-120

Race Discrimination 51
Retaliation 83-91
Romantic Relationships 120-123
    see also harassment, sex discrimination

Sex Discrimination (*see also* Harassment) 50-53

Slander (*see* Defamation)

Social Media 124-125
Statute of Limitations 63-65, 80-81, 136

Time Limits 63-65, 80-81, 136

Torts
  Defamation 27-39
  intentional infliction of emotional distress 18-20, 119-122
  intentional interference with a business expectancy 36-39
  privacy 117-122
  wrongful discharge 17-18

Unemployment 127-132
  Eligibility 128
  Misconduct 131-132

Whistleblower 51, 83-91
Wrongful Discharge 17-18

www.ingramcontent.com/pod-product-compliance
Lightning Source LLC
Chambersburg PA
CBHW051524170526
45165CB00002B/601